W9-AVZ-120

WOODWORKING PROJECTS

WITH A FEW BASIC HAND TOOLS

WOODWORKING PROJECTS

WITH A FEW BASIC HAND TOOLS

Michel Theriault

Sterling Publishing Co., Inc. New York

For my parents

Library of Congress Cataloging-in-Publication Data

Theriault, Michel, 1965–
    Woodworking projects with a few basic tools/Michel Theriault.
        p.   cm.
    Includes index.
    ISBN 0-8069-9469-X
    1. Woodwork.   2. Woodwork—Patterns.   3. House furnishings.
I. Title.
TT180.T47   1997
684'.08—dc21   97-40062
                                                                                CIP

10   9   8   7   6   5   4   3   2   1

Published by Sterling Publishing Company, Inc.
387 Park Avenue South, New York, N.Y. 10016
©1997 by Michel Theriault
Distributed in Canada by Sterling Publishing
c/o Canadian Manda Group, One Atlantic Avenue, Suite 105
Toronto, Ontario, Canada M6K 3E7
Distributed in Great Britain and Europe by Cassell PLC
Wellington House, 125 Strand, London WC2R 0BB, England
Distributed in Australia by Capricorn Link (Australia) Pty Ltd.

CONTENTS

ACKNOWLEDGMENTS

Special thanks to my loving wife Melanie and our sons, Chris and Jorden, for their patience, understanding, and support.

INTRODUCTION

This book challenges the common wisdom that you need a full range of tools and well-developed skills to make high-quality projects. While this may be true for large, complicated projects that require special joints and intricate construction, and have non-standard design dimensions, it doesn't have to be the rule. To make a carefully designed project, all you need are a few basic tools and the ability to perform some simple operations like measuring accurately and cutting straight.

In the following pages, you will learn to make an array of projects with basic hand tools. A list of such tools would include a handsaw, electric drill, jigsaw, hammer, screwdriver, hand plane, and miter box. Not every project will require all these tools. Some require only a handsaw and a hammer. In addition, you will need some accessories, such as a ruler, tape measure, square, and clamps. These tools and accessories represent a minimum investment in an enjoyable and exciting hobby. As with any hobby, as you get more experience and decide to build larger, more complicated projects, you will end up adding tools as you require them.

The first part of this book examines the essentials of project-making. This includes chapters on workshop considerations, the basic tools and accessories needed and their proper use, fastening materials and techniques, joint-making techniques, wood selection, and sanding and finishing techniques.

Next come instructions, tool and cutting lists, assembly drawings, and photos that show how to make over 30 useful projects. These projects include fold-up chairs, birdhouses, wall shelves, stools, toys, clocks, compact-disc holders, tool chests, benches, tables, and a children's activity center. I'm sure you will find some that appeal to you or some family member or will add a special touch to that favorite room in your house.

Michel Theriault

1
WORKSHOP CONSIDERATIONS

You don't need a dedicated workshop for woodworking. Simply make your projects wherever you can. Whether you live in a large house with a garage and basement or a small apartment, you can build woodworking projects. All you really need is an area to work in and some sort of work surface. Two main aspects to consider when deciding where to build your projects are sawdust and noise. These and others are discussed below.

SAWDUST

Sawdust is your greatest consideration when deciding where to build your projects. As long as you can sweep or vacuum it off the floor, you won't have a problem. A basement or garage is ideal for this. However, many of the projects are easily made in a kitchen or other room that doesn't have carpeting.

Using the basic tools listed, the amount of sawdust you generate will be relatively minor, and won't be fine enough to spread around the room and infiltrate nooks and crannies. Sanding, however, does make fine dust, so you should do it in a garage or in the backyard, especially if you

have added a power sander to your toolbox.

You can plan your project so that you create the sawdust where it won't be a problem, and complete the rest of the project somewhere else. This can be outside, in a garage, or in an unfinished basement. If you don't have a suitable place to work, or only have carpeted rooms, you could lay down a high-quality, durable drop sheet and build your project on it. It's a simple matter to clean up the drop sheet after you're done, and it will also prevent glue from dripping onto your floor.

NOISE

Power tools are the biggest contributors to noise when you are woodworking. The sound of a hammer driving nails is a close second. In our list of basic tools, the jigsaw will make the most noise. While it isn't noisy enough to bother the neighbors, it will certainly annoy family members who may be nearby. If this is the case and you are working where the noise may be disruptive, plan your project carefully so the noisy operations are carried out when they won't affect anyone else.

WORK SURFACE

A good, solid work surface is necessary when building your projects. While much of the work can even be done on the floor, you will need an elevated work surface for sawing and for convenience. The work surface could be the kitchen table, a workbench, sawhorses, or a portable bench. You don't have to limit yourself to a conventional workbench; anything that is very sturdy will work.

Traditional Workbench

Where you have a permanent area for woodworking, you may want to consider a traditional workbench, which is a sturdy bench built specifically for woodworking operations. The workbench project in this book (Illus. 1-1) is a simple, easy-to-construct workbench that is economical and sturdy. If you buy a commercially made workbench, make sure that it is very solid, with a surface that allows you to clamp all the way around its top and to saw on either side. Try to avoid a workbench that won't allow you to work on one or both sides, since this is where you will end up doing most of the sawing, either with a jigsaw or a handsaw.

Regardless of whether you build your own workbench or buy one, a vise is a useful accessory. You can buy a more expensive woodworking vise (Illus. 1-2) or a fairly inexpensive model (Illus. 1-3). The more expensive vise will have greater clamping capacity and strength, and features such as quick release and built-in bench dogs. Another option which falls in between expensive and inexpensive models is a traditional woodworking vise (Illus. 1-4), where you add your own handle and hardwood jaws.

Portable Workbench

A portable workbench is a good alternative when a full-size workbench isn't possible, or when you have very limited space in which to work. It also allows you to bring your shop to the work rather than bringing your work to the shop. There are a number of portable workbenches on the market. When shopping, don't buy one unless you can test it out in the store. You want to make sure it is very sturdy, well built, and quick and easy to assemble and to fold down for storage. One such workbench is the Workmate, by Black & Decker (Illus. 1-5).

Sawhorse

A sawhorse is a traditional work surface on which to rest your board while you saw or drill. It is simple, cheap, and versatile. You can bolt lengths of 2 × 4 or 2 × 6 boards together to make your own (Illus. 1-6) or buy one of several sawhorse brackets available and simply add lengths of 2 × 4 or 2 × 6 boards (Illus. 1-7–1-10). The brackets let you disassemble the sawhorse easily for storage. To make a portable workbench, you can place boards or a thick, wide panel between two sawhorses.

WORKSHOP SAFETY TECHNIQUES

Safety should be an important part of everything we do, and it needs to be applied even more diligently during woodworking, which involves sharp hand tools and powerful electric tools. Even though basic hand tools and portable power tools such as the

Illus. 1-1. This woodworking bench is easy to build. It is also sturdy. It is one of the projects described in Chapter 6.

Illus. 1-2. This large 9-inch vise has built-in dogs and a quick-release action.

Illus. 1-3. An inexpensive 6-inch vise.

Illus. 1-4. A traditional wood vise with 10-inch wooden jaws.

drill and jigsaw won't cause the same damage as a circular saw , table saw, or band saw, it is still important to reduce or eliminate the chance of

Illus. 1-5. This portable workbench will prove helpful if you are working in an area with very limited space.

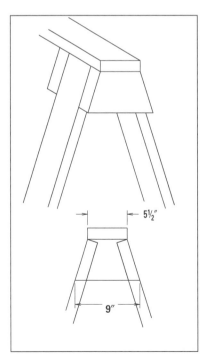

Illus. 1-6. A shop-made sawhorse without commercial brackets.

being cut. This means not just taking physical precautions, but also making sure you are alert. Never use tools when you are tired or can't think sharply or react quickly. As an added measure, keep a well-stocked first-aid kit within easy reach.

Always know where the cutting edge of a tool is and where it is going. Much of a jigsaw's blade is underneath the wood, where a finger can easily get in the way unless you

Illus. 1-7. Steel sawhorse brackets.

pay attention to the blade's path. A drill bit may start out on the top surface of your wood, yet once it's gone through, the pressure you are applying to the drill will suddenly drive the sharp, spinning bit well behind the wood. It is important to keep your hand or other body parts well away from its path.

Hand tools have a similar potential for danger. The plane has a very sharp blade, and an automatic and very careless gesture such as brushing shavings from the sole of the plane can cause a very bad cut. A screwdriver may seem like a very safe tool, yet if the tip slips off the screw head, it can easily puncture skin. The handsaw can create a very ragged cut if it is being carelessly used or stored. For safety and to keep your saws sharp, buy blade guards for them.

The three most important areas of concern when woodworking should

Illus. 1-8. This sawhorse uses steel brackets.

always be your hearing, vision, and lungs. Woodworking can potentially damage all three if suitable precau- tions are not taken. Hearing protec- tion isn't needed when you are using hand tools. However, the noise creat- ed by many power tools can cause permanent damage to your hearing if you don't protect against it, because its effects can be cumulative. Earmuffs or earplugs (Illus. 1-11) are the best defense for your hearing. Sawdust can not only damage your lungs, but it is possible to develop an allergic reaction to some woods after prolonged exposure to sawdust. A face mask can be either a simple dis- posable paper mask (Illus. 1-12) or a rubber face mask with a filter car- tridge (Illus. 1-13). Eye protection (Illus. 1-14) is imperative, since eyes are an exposed and vulnerable part of the body, and are usually pointed directly at the work, exposing them to the risk of flying splinters, large particles of sawdust, and flying chips of metal from broken bits. Special shatterproof prescription glasses are available if necessary, or you can use a pair of goggles over your own glasses. If you don't already wear glasses, you can use a pair of safety glasses instead of goggles.

You should also be safety-con-

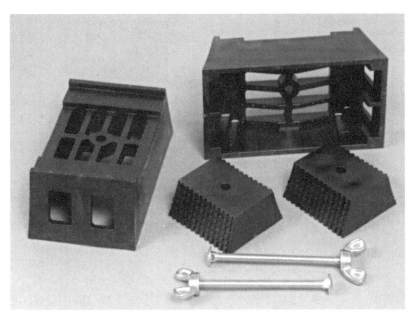

Illus. 1-9. Plastic sawhorse brackets.

Illus. 1-10. This sawhorse uses plastic brackets.

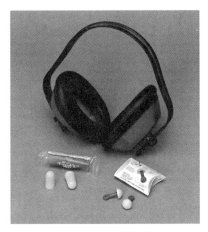

Illus. 1-11. Woodworkers should always wear some form of ear protection. Shown here are earmuffs and two types of ear plugs.

scious when staining or finishing your completed project. Stains and finishes should always be used in well-ventilated areas, and you should avoid inhaling any fumes from the finish, even when it is designated as low-odor or environmentally friendly. Skin contact can also be dangerous, not to mention unpleasant, so always use rubber or vinyl gloves. Protect your eyes from splashes by wearing safety glasses or goggles.

If you need to use an extension cord with your electric tool, be sure to use the appropriate one. A round, jacketed cord should always be used, since it provides added protection in a workshop where it can be easily abused. Also, the longer the cord and larger the motor size, the larger the wire size must be, to avoid damaging your tool or creating a fire hazard (Table 1-1).

Illus. **1-12**. A disposable paper face mask.

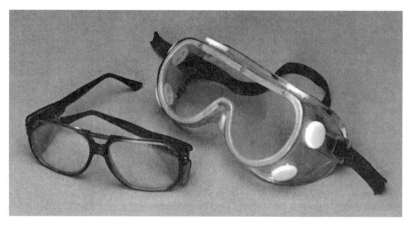

Illus. **1-14**. Your eyes are very vulnerable when you are woodworking, so wear eye protection. Shown here are goggles and safety glasses.

Illus. **1-13**. A rubber face mask with a filter cartridge.

Cord Length (round jacket only)	Wire Gauge					
	Up to 2A	2A to 3.5A	3.5A to 5A	5A to 7A	7A to 12A	12A to 16A
Up to 25 feet	16	16	16	16	14	14
25 to 50 feet	16	16	16	14	14	14
50 to 100 feet	16	16	14	12	10	

Table **1-1**. Extension cord limits. An undersized extension cord can result in loss of power and overheating, possibly damaging your tool.

2

BASIC TOOLS AND WORKSHOP AIDS

ELECTRIC DRILL

When you take advantage of the wide variety of different accessories available for use with the electric drill, you can transform it into the most versatile of the hand tools. Most manufacturers make consumer models that are well priced yet have the features you need (Illus. 2-1–2-3). While the higher-priced models, including the industrial versions, are built better and will last longer, the occasional user isn't likely to notice a significant difference in design and construction. However, if you expect to use your drill constantly now or in the future, you may want to invest in a higher-end or industrial version.

When shopping for a drill, don't settle for one that won't meet your foreseeable needs. A single-speed drill may seem an economical choice; however, once you begin using it, you will quickly recognize its limitations compared with a variable-speed drill. Variable-speed drills (Illus. 2-4) come in a variety of rpm ranges, from 0–600 rpm to 0–3,000 rpm. For general woodworking, you should have a drill with a higher maximum rpm, usually with a top end in the 2,000 to 2,500 rpm range. This allows the higher speeds that drilling holes with small-diameter bits demands, and provides the speed necessary for some accessories such as flap or drum sanders to work best. In almost all cases, variable-speed drills are also reversible; however, it is best to check for this feature before buying a drill. Reversible speed allows you to remove screws and back a jammed drill bit out of the hole.

Whether to buy a corded or cordless drill is largely a matter of your specific need. If you expect to need a drill where you don't have ready access to electricity, then a cordless drill (Illus. 2-5) is the answer. If you will be using it exclusively in your basement or garage where electric outlets are close by, then the added expense may not be justifiable. The capacities of today's cordless drills are excellent as long as you buy a quality drill with a large battery

Illus. 2-1. This electric drill has a keyless chuck and reversible variable speed.

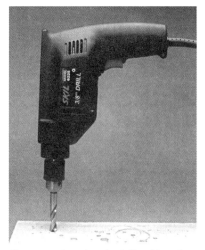

Illus. 2-2. An electric drill with a key chuck.

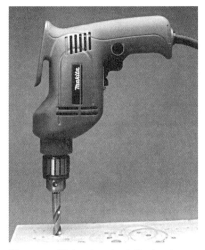

Illus. 2-3. This electric drill also has a key chuck.

pack. If you expect to use it a lot, be sure to buy a spare battery pack and keep it charged just in case your first battery runs out in the middle of a job. Cordless drills typically come with one feature not usually found on a corded drill—a clutch (Illus. 2-6). This allows you to dial up a particular torque, and the drill will automatically disengage when it reaches the limit, a feature which is useful when you are driving screws.

Electric drills come in three typical sizes: $1/4$, $3/8$, and $1/2$ inch. These sizes refer to the largest-diameter shank that can be gripped by the drill's chuck. The size of the motor and the power available are also often related to the chuck size; the $1/2$-inch drills typically are much stronger and have a larger drilling capacity than the $1/4$-inch drills. For woodworking, a $3/8$-inch drill is a good choice, since it is generally

powerful enough, and most drill bits for woodworking have a $3/8$-inch-or-less shank, regardless of their size.

The chuck is the business end of a drill (Illus. 2-7–2-9). It is either tightened with a key or is "keyless," which means it is specially designed to be tightened by hand. The keyless chucks make the drill slightly more expensive. However, they work very well, and are quite convenient to use. It is possible to buy a keyless chuck to replace an existing key chuck, if desired. A less expensive alternative is to add specially made rubber rings (Illus. 2-10) to the key chuck, which will allow the chuck to act like a keyless chuck. The rings work well, but don't have the holding power of a real keyless chuck.

Another consideration is the size of the motor, usually rated in amperage. All other things being equal, the higher the number of amps, the more powerful the drill will be. The

Illus. 2-4. A close-up of the trigger on a reversible variable speed drill.

Illus. 2-6. A close-up of a typical clutch on a cordless drill.

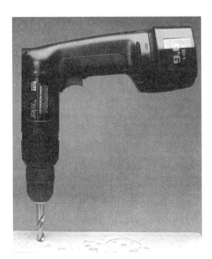

Illus. 2-5. This cordless drill has a keyless chuck.

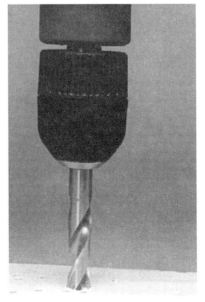

Illus. 2-7. A close-up of a keyless chuck.

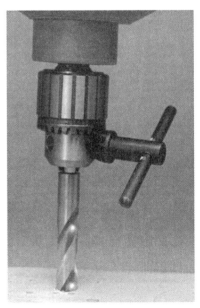

Illus. 2-8. A close-up of a key chuck with the key in place.

gearing and speeds also are factors that influence the power of a drill, since a drill with a very high maximum speed will stall more easily than a drill with a very low maximum speed. A large motor will also stand up better under tough or continuous drilling conditions without overheating.

Using a Drill

The drill can be used with one hand; however, it is best to use two, for extra support and control. Some larger models have a handle attached to the body of the drill with which you can steady the drill and help apply pressure. Holding your drill with both hands (Illus. 2-11) will help prevent a sprained wrist if your bit digs in and the drill begins twisting. For a similar reason, make sure your wood is firmly clamped or held down while you drill. You can get hurt if the drill catches on or encounters a little extra resistance from a knot and sends your wood spinning.

Drilling straight holes (Illus. 2-12) is the biggest challenge with a hand-held electric drill. This is essential for good construction, and can be done with practice and a little bit of attention. With many drill bits such as the spade, Forstner, and brad-point bits, you can see the diameter of the hole being cut away first as the bit enters the wood (Illus. 2-13 and 2-14). This can give you an idea of how straight your hole is, and give you time to adjust the drill to get a straight hole before you have gone very far. To keep the drill straight, keep an eye on the drill and the shaft of the drill bit to ensure you aren't allowing the drill to wander. A feature built into some drills is a level that can be used as a reference for keeping the drill straight (Illus. 2-15). There are also a number of accessories available (which will be covered later) to help you get straight holes.

Starting your hole accurately is very important for good construction, especially when using dowels. Use a pencil or scribe to mark a cross at the center of the hole before drilling. To be sure your drill bit doesn't wander and stays on your mark when you begin drilling, use a center punch or large nail to create a dimple in the middle of your mark.

For the sake of your drill, don't apply any more pressure than necessary while drilling. You will know how much is enough with some practice and a few basic guidelines. First, start slowly when drilling and apply light pressure on the drill. Increase the speed slowly until the bit is cutting well without straining or burning the wood. You should let the drill work for you, so don't lean into it heavily. You will always need to apply some pressure, but if you need to lean on your drill, it is a sure sign of a dull drill bit.

The type of wood and size of your drill bit will dictate the best speed for drilling. Typically, the larger the diameter of the bit, the slower the speed. You will eventually get the feel for the right speed as you gain experience. With large-diameter drill bits in particular, too high a

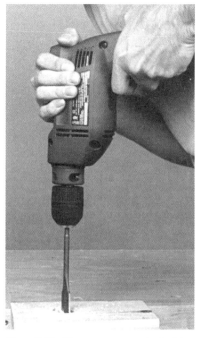

Illus. 2-11. The proper way to hold a drill, to ensure safety and accuracy.

Illus. 2-9. A standard key chuck on a drill, and a replacement chuck to convert the drill into a keyless chuck.

Illus. 2-10. Rubber rings are available to convert a key chuck into a keyless chuck. This method is not as good as buying an actual keyless chuck; however, it is less expensive.

speed can also overheat the drill bit, causing it to lose its temper. If this happens, it won't keep a sharp edge and will become dull quickly. One way to avoid overheating your drill bit for deep or large-diameter holes is to withdraw it periodically from the hole. At the same time, you can remove the sawdust and wood chips from the hole and from the flutes on the drill.

Electric Drill Accessories

Drill bits Woodworkers have a wide range of drill bits to select from (Illus. 2-16). Depending on your budget and the specific application, you can use standard metal twist drills, spade bits (flat bits), Forstner bits, brad-point bits (also known as dowel bits), or hole saws.

(Although the hole saw is a blade rather than a bit, it is included in this section on bits.)

There are several factors to consider when choosing a drill bit, including the drill's shank size, the diameter and depth of the hole, whether the hole will go all the way through the wood, and the drilling accuracy required. The drill bit's shank size should fit your drill. Most woodworking bits will have a shank of $3/8$ inch or less, which is ideal for a $3/8$-inch or larger drill. However,

Illus. 2-13. With some drill bits, you can see how straight your bit is as it enters the wood.

some brands of drill bit start a set of bits with one size shank and jump to a larger shank on larger drill bits.

The hole sizes you expect to drill can also guide your choice of drill bits (Table 2-1). For smaller holes such as pilot holes for screws, the standard twist drill is ideal, while very large holes will require an expensive Forstner bit or less expensive hole saw.

All types of drill bit except hole saws can drill fairly deep holes, usually deep enough to be able to go all the way through wood when necessary. Generally, the length of the drill bit increases with its diameter, and adapters are available which can extend this depth by several inches. Hole saws are limited by the depth inside the saw blade. They typically only allow you to drill a hole through material that is $3/4$ inch thick or less.

For stopped holes or holes which don't go all the way through your wood, each type of drill bit will leave a different bottom (Illus. 2-17 and 2-18). For many projects, this may not be important. However, you should be aware of the differences. The only

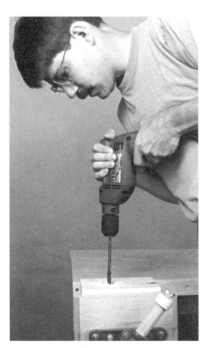

Illus. 2-12. Drilling straight holes with an electric drill.

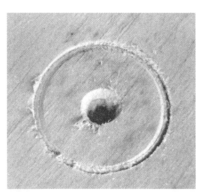

Illus. 2-14. A close-up of the marks made by a spade bit as it enters the wood.

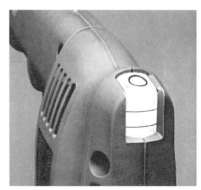

Illus. 2-15. The level built into this drill is used as a reference for keeping the drill straight.

drill bit that can't drill stopped holes is the hole saw.

Where a clean, accurate hole is required, a Forstner bit is the best to use, with the brad-point bit close behind. The spade bit will do a reasonable job if it is very sharp and held perfectly straight.

Metal Twist Drill Metal twist drills are available in both carbon and high-speed steel (Illus. 2-19 and 2-20). High-speed-steel (HSS) bits will stay sharp longer, but may not be worth the extra cost for occasional use. These bits are most suited to small-diameter holes such as pilot holes. For this reason, a small inexpensive set ranging from $\frac{1}{16}$ to $\frac{1}{4}$ inch would be the best choice.

Brad-Point Drill Bits While similar in nature to twist drill bits, brad-point bits (Illus. 2-21 and 2-22) are specifically designed for wood. They feature a deeper gullet, a distinct center spur, and edge spurs to ensure an accurate hole with a clean entry. They are available in carbon steel and high-speed steel. HSS brad-point bits will stay sharp longer and give a slightly better cut. Another variation that is important to note when buying them is the design of their tips. Utility-grade bits will have edge spurs that are less defined and not as sharp as a higher-quality bit. This can affect the quality of the entry hole. These drills are also called dowel bits because they are commonly used to drill dowel holes.

When using a brad-point drill bit, remember that it is quite aggressive and can easily dig in if you don't keep a light yet steady pressure. If the bit digs in, reverse the drill and back the bit out.

Spade Bits As a low-cost bit designed for wood only, spade bits (Illus. 2-23 and 2-24) typically scrape the wood rather than cut it. Some newer designs act more like a cutting bit; however, the key to using them

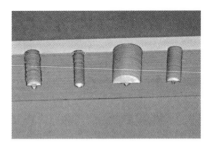

Illus. 2-17. Different bits leave different shapes on the bottom of holes. Shown here, from left to right, are holes made by a utility brad-point bit, spiral bit, a Forstner bit, and a high-speed-steel brad-point bit.

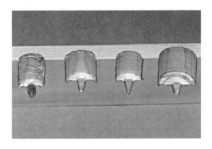

Illus. 2-18. From left to right are holes made by a lead screw bit, a spade bit with spurs, a spade bit without spurs, and an adjustable spade bit.

Illus. 2-16. A selection of drill bits.

Type of Drill Bit	Size range
Twist drill bits	$\frac{1}{16}$ to $\frac{1}{2}$ inch
Brad point bits	$\frac{1}{8}$ to $\frac{1}{2}$ inch
Spade bits	$\frac{3}{8}$ to $1\frac{1}{5}$ inches
Expansive spade bits	$\frac{5}{8}$ to 3 inches
Forstner Bits	$\frac{1}{4}$ to $2\frac{1}{8}$ inches
Hole saws	$\frac{1}{2}$ to $2\frac{1}{2}$ inches

Table 2-1. This chart shows the drill bit size range available for each of the drill bit types. Note that both larger and smaller sizes may be available for special applications.

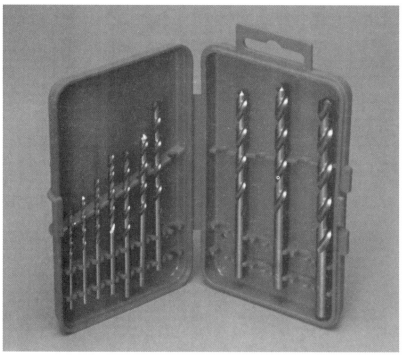

Illus. 2-19. A twist drill-bit set.

satisfactorily is still to make sure they are kept very sharp. Because the bits are long and their shafts are relatively thin, be sure not to bend the bit while you are using it.

If you buy a set of spade bits, be sure to choose a high-quality set. Typically, a set will contain bits ranging from $\frac{3}{8}$ to 1 inch in diameter. Larger bits are available individually, and it may be more economical to buy the larger bits as you need them.

The design of the cutting end of spade bits can vary. For the smoothest entry hole and a better cut, buy the winged versions rather than the flat-bottom ones. When using the bit to drill blind or stopped holes, be aware of its long center spur. If you don't take this center spur into account, it may create a hole where you don't want one. When drilling with spade bits, you

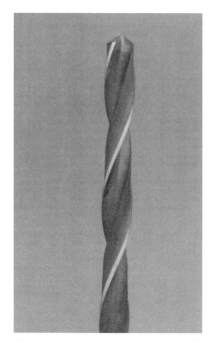

Illus. 2-20. A typical metal twist drill bit.

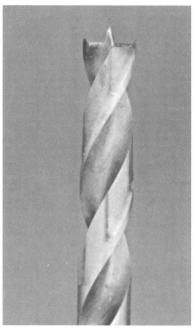

Illus. 2-21. A high-speed-steel brad-point drill bit.

Illus. 2-22. A utility-grade brad-point drill bit.

will need to apply more pressure and drill at a higher speed than with other drill bits, due to their scraping action. One benefit is that since they don't have a spiral and don't cut, they are less likely to dig in when you are drilling. However, since they don't have a spiral to remove the wood chips from the hole while you are drilling, you will have to stop and clean out the hole periodically.

A variation of the spade bit is the expansive bit (Illus. 2-25). When used with one or more interchangeable cutters, this bit allows you to drill a wide range of hole sizes that are infinitely adjustable. One drawback of this method is that getting an accurate hole size requires a little trial and error, since the scale built onto the cutters is seldom accurate enough.

Forstner Bits Specifically designed for woodworking, these bits come in a wide range of sizes, from $1/4$ through 3 inches in diameter (Illus. 2-26). They create a clean, accurate hole with a relatively flat bottom. The design of their rim allows them to cut holes at an angle or where one edge of the hole is off the wood. Because of their design, they should be used at slow speeds. They perform best in a drill press; however, when used with a steady hand, they are fine for drilling freehand.

Hole Saws The hole saw is not really a bit. It is a band-saw-type blade formed into a circle and mounted onto a drill (Illus. 2-27 and 2-28). Carbon steel blades are commonly used, but the more expensive bi-metal blades will last much longer. They can be bought as individual pieces or in a set. Most hole saws have interchangeable blades and a single mandrel. However, it is possible to get hole saws that are of one piece. Typically, you would require two different-size mandrels to accommodate the entire range of hole-saw sizes.

Since hole saws cut around the rim of the hole only, a drill bit is used in the center of the hole saw. The bit is attached to the mandrel, which allows you to start the hole in its center and to keep the saw from wandering until it is properly started. Hole saws will not allow you to drill blind or stopped holes, and are limited in the depth they can cut. The resulting plug cut by a hole saw can be used as a wheel for toys. It even has a built-in axle hole.

When using a hole saw, it is important to ensure that it goes into the wood straight and is kept straight while cutting. Be sure to use an appropriate speed. If you drill too fast, you can overheat the saw, especially when cutting hard wood. When drilling to the hole saw's depth capacity, withdraw the hole saw periodically to clear out the sawdust.

Leadscrew Drill Bit The leadscrew drill bit actually has a screw-type point at its end that pulls the bit into the wood as it is used. This bit is very suitable for quick, rough

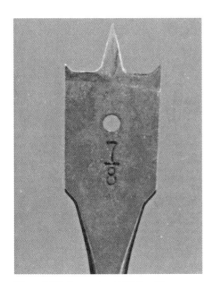

Illus. 2-23. A spade drill bit with spurs.

Illus. 2-24. A spade drill bit without spurs.

Illus. 2-25. An expandable spade drill bit.

Illus. 2-26. A Forstner drill bit.

Illus. 2-27. Shown here is a hole-saw set with a mandrel, and a hole saw mounted on a drill.

Illus. 2-28. An adjustable hole saw mounted on a drill.

holes. However, it does not produce clean, accurate holes (Illus. 2-29).

Flap and Drum Sanders Drum sanders (Illus. 2-30) are an inexpensive yet vital drill accessory for any

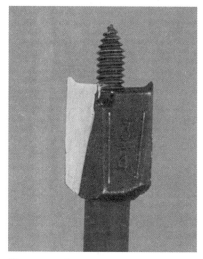

Illus. 2-29. This leadscrew drill bit can be used to quickly drill rough holes.

project that uses a jigsaw. The drum sander allows you to sand the curved edge cut by the jigsaw much more evenly and efficiently than by hand.

Drum sanders are available in diameters from $\frac{1}{2}$ to 2 inches and in lengths from 1 to 2 inches. They normally have a $\frac{1}{4}$-inch shank, which is suitable for any drill. Sanding sleeves are simply slipped over a rubber cylinder and a nut squeezes the rubber to hold the sleeve in place. They are available in grits that range from #80 to #120.

When using a drum sander to sand edges, use a high speed and keep the drum perpendicular to the work. Move it along the wood in the direction opposite from the drill's direction of rotation. Otherwise, the drum sander will pull itself along the wood and will be harder to control.

The flap sander (Illus. 2-31) is an alternative to the drum sander. Since it isn't rigid like a drum sander, the flap sander will result in a softer

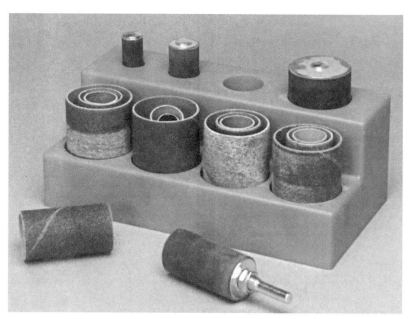

Illus. 2-30. A drum sander set.

curve. Flap sanders are typically of a finer grit than drum sanders, so are a good choice for finish-sanding on curved edges.

The best way to use a flap or drum sander is to mount the drill in a commercial drill stand (Illus. 2-32 and 2-33) or make your own basic stand to clamp your drill to the workbench.

Illus. 2-31. A flap sander mounted in a drill.

Screw-Hole Formers Screw-hole formers (Illus. 2-34 and 2-35) come in a wide variety of styles and can be indispensable if you construct projects using screws. You can drill the pilot and clearance holes, counterbore, and countersinks in one operation. Most formers are adjustable. While it is possible to do all this with several twist drills and a single countersink bit, the low cost and versatility of the specialized hole formers is worth it.

It is necessary to use a hole former sized properly for the screws you are using (head size/shank diameter). Otherwise, you will end up with a poor joint or the screw simply won't fit. If you use a variety of screw sizes, then a set may be the best option. If you use one size exclusively, it is more economical to buy the size you need. Screw formers are usually identified for use with specific screw sizes, such as #6, #8, or #10.

Choosing the right screw-hole former will depend on how you

expect to use it. For counterboring or countersinking only, then a former that is "fixed" will perform best. For a variety of tasks, the adjustable versions have a depth stop which will allow you to drill holes that are either counterbored or countersunk, and will allow you to vary the depth of the counterbore.

Some formers can be changed quickly, which permits you to switch between the former and the screw-driving bit without much effort (Illus. 2-36–2-38). This is quite convenient if you want to screw the parts of the project together as you drill the pilot holes, rather than drilling all the pilot holes first.

HANDSAW

Your handsaw will be the most important tool you use. It allows you to accurately cut your wood to the right length or to cut straight angles for projects. Most of the cutting you

Illus. 2-32. This flap sander and drill are mounted on a drill stand.

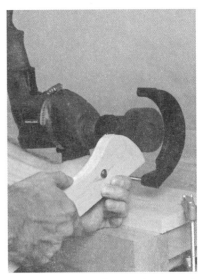

Illus. 2-33. Using a flap sander to sand a jigsawn contour.

do with a handsaw for the projects in this book will be crosscuts (across the grain) (Illus. 2-39), rather than rip cuts (with the grain) (Illus. 2-40 and 2-41), so a good handsaw with fine teeth is a requirement.

There are actually two important variations of the handsaw: the traditional handsaw and the backsaw. Handsaws (Illus. 2-42) are often called panel saws because they are made from a flat piece of saw blade and can cut through a long panel, leaving a thin kerf behind. Backsaws (Illus. 2-43) have a rigid back at the top of a rectangular blade which makes the blade very stiff. The back, however, prevents the blade from cutting far into a piece of wood or plywood. The quality of cut is large-ly based on the number of teeth per inch on the blade. Ripsaws generally have 5 teeth per inch (tpi), while crosscut saws range from 7 to 11 tpi. Backsaws are specifically designed for crosscutting, and typically those with the highest number of teeth per inch give the best cuts. The backsaw is only suitable for crosscutting standard-width boards, and is often used with a miter box. You can substitute a regular handsaw in place of a backsaw for almost any application if necessary, such as when using a miter box. However, you won't be assured of quite as smooth, straight, and even a cut.

Handsaws come in a variety of

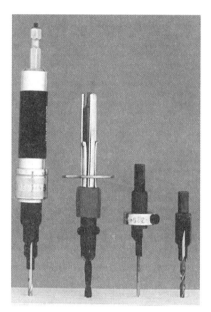

Illus. 2-34. Screw-hole formers for pilot holes.

Illus. 2-36. Two quick-change screw-hole formers.

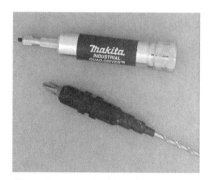

Illus. 2-37. A Makita quick-change screw-hole former.

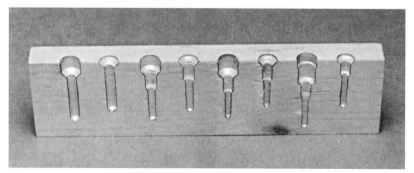

Illus. 2-35. The counterbored and countersunk profiles for the screw-hole formers shown in Illus. 2-34. These profiles are shown in reverse order of the formers in Illus. 2-34.

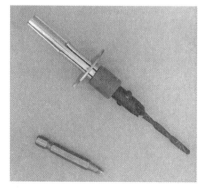

Illus. 2-38. A utility quick-change screw-hole former.

Illus. **2-39**. Crosscutting with a handsaw.

Illus. **2-40**. Ripping with a handsaw.

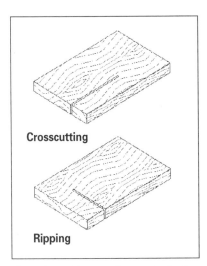

Crosscutting

Ripping

Illus. **2-41**. Crosscutting and ripping cuts.

lengths (Illus. 2-44 and 2-45), from the toolbox-size 15-inch handsaw to handsaws with a standard length of 26 inches. Backsaws range in length from 14 to 16 inches.

Handsaws come in a wide range of tooth types. Three basic types of teeth are standard, chisel, and hardpoint teeth (Illus. 2-46–2-49).

Handsaws with standard teeth are basic saws that cut well. They can be easily resharpened. Those with hardpoint teeth are specially tempered, will cut aggressively, and will remain quite sharp indefinitely with proper care, which is important since they cannot be resharpened. Those with chisel teeth cut either on the

Illus. **2-42**. A standard-tooth panel saw or handsaw.

Illus. **2-43**. A backsaw with standard teeth.

Illus. **2-44**. A short handsaw with bevel-cutting teeth.

Illus. **2-45**. A short handsaw with hardpoint teeth.

pull or push stroke, and cut very aggressively and cleanly.

Using Your Handsaw

Getting a straight cut from a handsaw is largely a matter of proper body position and careful attention to the saw as it cuts. By positioning your body properly, it will be easy to keep the saw on a straight line, producing not only a straight cut, but an even, smooth surface. Your hand, shoulder, and elbow should be in line, allowing you to guide the saw through the strokes without requiring an effort to keep it straight.

In addition to keeping the cut straight and on line, don't allow it to tilt to one side or the other. This could create a joint with gaps because the cut surface won't be perfectly square or straight (Illus. 2-50).

To start the cut, position the saw on the wood just to the waste side of your mark (Illus. 2-51). The handle should be close to the wood. With a gentle pull stroke, create an indent to guide the saw, and then begin sawing with a smooth, firm stroke.

Apply slight pressure on the push stroke, letting up on the pull stroke. Since the saw cuts on the push stroke, the good side of your wood should be facing up so any splintering will be on the bottom.

When finishing a cut, slow down the saw and ease up any pressure, to avoid creating a splinter at the last corner as the cut is completed. Also, be sure to support the waste side so that the weight of the piece won't break off the wood before it is completely cut through (Illus. 2-52).

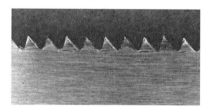

Illus. 2-46. A close-up of the standard teeth on a handsaw.

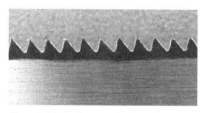

Illus. 2-47. A close-up look at the hard-point teeth on a handsaw.

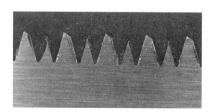

Illus. 2-48. A close-up look at bevel-cutting chisel teeth on a handsaw.

Illus. 2-49. A handsaw with hard-point teeth.

Illus. 2-50. Crosscutting along a line with a handsaw.

SCREWDRIVERS

While screwdrivers are essential for turning screws into wood, you will probably only use hand screwdrivers when your power drivers can't reach a screw, or to install hardware with brass screws that are easily damaged by power drivers. Power drivers chucked in a drill are more a necessity than a luxury, considering the low price of power-driver bits.

Screwdriver sets (Illus. 2-53 and 2-54) usually contain several screw-drivers that accommodate different sizes and types of screw head, or one multi-bit screwdriver with different types and sizes of bit. Common types of screwdriver are slotted, Phillips, and Robertson (square-drive) heads. Other specialty screws are rarely used in woodworking. The flathead screwdriver is for brass screws that are commonly used with hardware and come in very small sizes. Phillips and Robertson screw-drivers are the primary ones used for wood screws (Illus. 2-55).

When looking for a screwdriver, select one with large handles. This allows you to get a good grip. Just as important are good-quality, tempered ends. Some types of slotted and Phillips screwdriver have serrat-

Illus. 2-51. Starting a cut with a hand-saw.

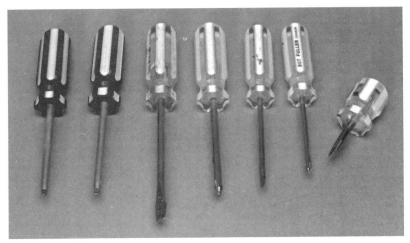

Illus. 2-53. A set of screwdrivers with Phillips, Robertson, and straight heads.

Illus. 2-52. This piece broke off be-cause the waste side of the cut was not supported.

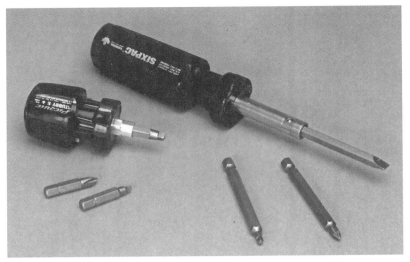

Illus. 2-54. Regular and stubby multi-bit screwdrivers. The bits are stored in the handles.

ed tips that provide a positive grip while driving screws, because slotted and Phillips screwdrivers have a tendency to "cam-out" while driving screws unless you use a great downward force. The Robertson screwdriver does not have this tendency.

Power Drivers

Power drivers (Illus. 2-56) are bits designed to be chucked in a drill for driving screws. They range from 1 to 3 inches in length and come in the same bit sizes as those for hand screwdrivers. They are indispensable when you are driving lots of screws or when working with a hard wood such as maple, because they provide a quick, effortless way to drive screws.

Using Power Drivers When using a power driver, it is important to ensure you don't strip the screw hole or shear off the head. When using a variable-speed drill, slow down its speed as the screw is seated and just drive the screw into the wood until it is tight and snug. If you use a power driver for brass screws, drive the screw until just before it is seated; then use a hand screwdriver to tighten the screw. Otherwise, you risk damaging the head of the screw or shearing it right off.

HAMMERS

Although the hammer's primary job is to drive nails, it is also used to remove nails and serve as a mallet if you don't own one. While the construction on most larger projects isn't likely to use nails, there are many smaller projects where nails

are quite useful.

Claw hammers (Illus. 2-57) are available in many different weights. The weight of the one you choose should depend on the use the hammer will get and the size of nail it is expected to drive. A 16-ounce hammer provides enough weight to drive nails without too much effort, and it is not too heavy to use comfortably. The type of handle is largely a matter of personal preference. Handles range from conventional wooden handles to rubber-covered steel handles to fiberglass composite handles.

Using Your Hammer

When hammering nails, position your body and hammer in such a way that the head of the hammer will be perfectly flat when it hits the nail head. Adjust your body as the nail is driven into the wood. If you strike the nail and it bends, hit it on the side with your hammer until it is straight

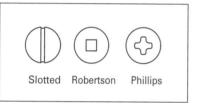

Slotted   Robertson   Phillips

Illus. 2-55. Slotted, Phillips, and Robertson head designs.

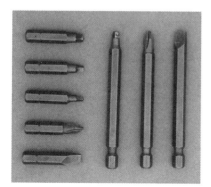

Illus. 2-56. Examples of power-driver bits.

Illus. 2-57. On top is a standard wooden-handled claw hammer. Below it is a professional all-steel claw hammer.

again and resume hammering. Ease up on the force when the nail is almost flush with the wood, to avoid damaging the wood. If you are driving finishing nails, use a nail set or another nail to drive the head of the finishing nail about $\frac{1}{16}$ inch beneath the surface of the wood, so it is ready to be filled in with plastic wood.

To pull nails, force the claw of the hammer underneath the nail head and pry it upwards. This will invariably damage the wood, but there is no real alternative. For longer nails, use a block of wood under the claw for additional leverage once the nail has been pulled out partway.

MITER BOXES

The miter box (Illus. 2-58–2-61) is essential for cutting precise 90- and 45-degree angles on narrow boards or molding. It provides for several preset angles and guides the saw while you cut. There are several types of miter box, ranging from simple wooden boxes to high-end metal versions that use specialized saws.

You can buy either a wooden or plastic version of the traditional miter box. This is a simple U-shaped device into which you place your wood . The front and back have slots which allow you to select either a right (90-degree) angle cut or a mitered (45-degree) cut in either direction. Because of the way miter boxes are constructed, there is a limit to the maximum width of wood you can miter, which is usually about 4 inches, although some models will accommodate a wider board. They are usually used with a backsaw. However, a small handsaw will also work. When a miter box is used constantly, its slots will wear out, reduc-

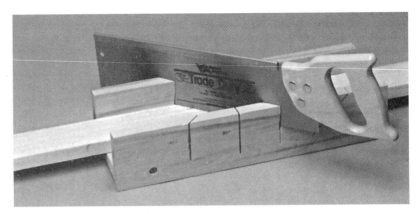

Illus. 2-58. A wooden miter box.

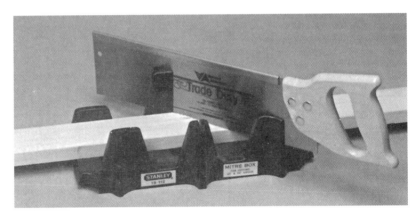

Illus. 2-59. A plastic miter box.

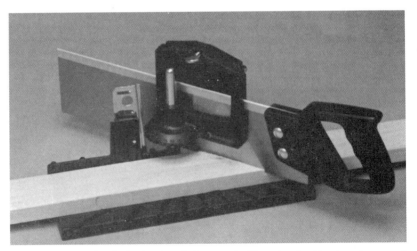

Illus. 2-60. A mechanical miter box being used with a standard backsaw or panel saw.

ing its accuracy. When this happens, you need to replace the box.

The mechanical boxes range widely in price, from the economical to the high-end professional models that cost almost as much as power miter boxes. A simple mechanical box uses an indexed saw holder which accommodates either a backsaw or handsaw and allows a larger range of angles to be cut. It is more accurate than the ordinary version, and the maximum width of your cut isn't as limited, depending on its design. Another version of the mechanical miter box uses a special bow saw that has a very thin kerf and is kept straight with special guides for the most accurate miter cuts.

You can use a miter box to cut a miter on either the face or edge of the wood (Illus. 2-62), as long as you are within the limits of the miter box. If not, you will have to cut the miters freehand. To cut a face miter with a miter box, lay your piece flat on the bottom of the miter box and hold it tightly against its back. Saw with your blade quite flat on the top of the wood. Use smooth, even strokes. Some miter boxes have a bottom ledge on the front of the box which is meant to hang over the front of a workbench to prevent the miter box from moving.

When cutting straight 90-degree angles, holding the wood with your hand is often sufficient. When you are cutting a miter, your miter box or even the wood can easily shift because you are putting pressure on it at the angle of the miter. In this case, it is best to clamp the wood and miter box to your workbench.

HAND PLANES

While there are dozens of different types of planes available for hand-work, there are two basic varieties that should be considered first. These are the **block** and **smoothing** planes (Illus. 2-63). A smoothing plane is about $9 \frac{1}{2}$ inches long and $1\frac{3}{4}$ inches wide. Its primary use is to smoothen flat surfaces and to joint the edges of boards, by either cleaning up saw marks or preparing the edges for a glue-up. A block plane is designed for use on end grain. It can be used to smoothen and square up the end of a board after it has been cut with a handsaw. It is smaller than a smoothing plane, and its blade is at a much shallower angle than a smoothing plane's blade, so it cuts end grain better.

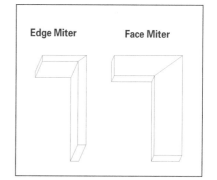

Illus. 2-62. Face and edge miters.

Illus. 2-61. A mechanical miter box being used with a special bow saw.

Illus. 2-63. A block plane (foreground) and smoothing plane.

Even though planes can be used to take a rough board down to finished dimensions, this takes lots of practice and time. We will limit the discussion of using hand planes to cleaning up the surface of edge-glued boards, preparing cut surfaces for jointing, simply cleaning up saw marks, and planing a bevel on the edge of a board.

With all planes, proper adjustment is critical to successful planing. Follow the instructions that come with your plane closely, noting the different settings which may be required, depending on the use.

Using Your Plane

When planing the flat surface of a board as, for example, smoothening the surface between two glued-up boards, always plane in the direction of the grain, holding the plane at a slight angle (Illus. 2-64). If the plane is catching in the grain, you may need to change direction (Illus. 2-65). To ensure a flat, even surface, apply more pressure at the front of the plane when beginning a stroke and at the back of the plane when ending a stroke. Set a straightedge or ruler on its edge across the board with a

strong light behind it to check for flatness. The light coming through under the edge will show you where more planing is necessary.

When planing an edge, it is important to hold the plane square to the face of the board (Illus. 2-66). Check your progress frequently with a square and use this as a guide to adjust how you hold your plane. If planing a fairly wavy edge that was cut with a jigsaw or handsaw, mark a guideline from the straight edge of the board by measuring the width from the straight edge at regular intervals, and then joining the marks with a ruler.

If planing a specific chamfer or bevel (Illus. 2-67 and 2-68), mark the exact chamfer or bevel at each end of the board and join these marks with one line along the face of the board. This will serve as a guide when you plane down to the angle.

While you can use a smoothing plane for planing the ends (end grain) of your boards (Illus. 2-69), the low angle of a block plane makes it ideal for this job (Illus. 2-70). A careful, smooth cut from a good, sharp handsaw will often be enough; however, you may sometimes need to

Illus. 2-64. Planing a glued-up board flat with a smoothing plane.

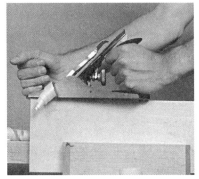

Illus. 2-66. Planing an edge with a smoothing plane.

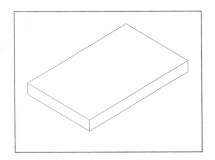

Illus. 2-65. When planing the flat surface of the board, plane in the direction of the grain.

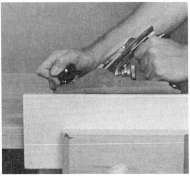

Illus. 2-67. Planing a bevel on the edge of a board with a smoothing plane.

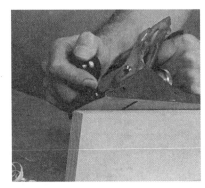

Illus. 2-68. A close-up of the bevel being planed with a smoothing plane.

A GALLERY OF WOOD PROJECTS

KITCHEN PROJECTS

a. Spice Rack

b. Recipe Book Holder

c. Kitchen Keeper

d. Cutting Board

HOUSEHOLD PROJECTS

e. CD Holder

f. Night Table

g. Wall Shelf

h. Display Cabinet

i. Clock

j. Firewood Box

k. Mail Box

OUTDOOR PROJECTS

l. Window Planter   **p.** Patio Table

m. Garden Planter   **q.** Garden Bench

n. Bird Feeder   **r.** Fold-Up Chair

o. Birdhouse

CHILDREN'S PROJECTS

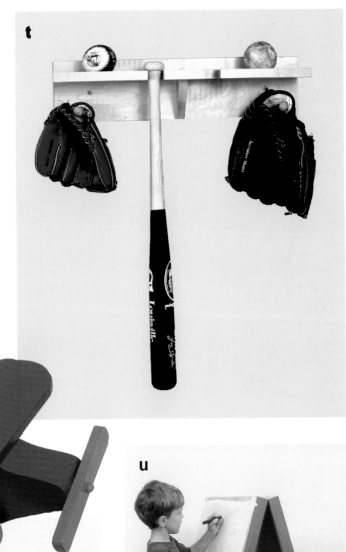

x

SHOP PROJECTS

x. Workbench

y. Tool Chest

z. Tool Box

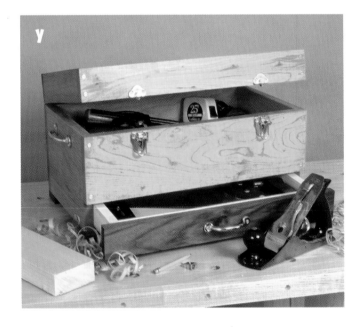

y

z

clean up the cut or make it perfectly smooth for a better joint. As with planing an edge, you must hold the plane square to the face of the board. To eliminate the possibility of causing splits in the edges, always start your stroke at the edge and end it before reaching the far side (Illus. 2-71). Repeat this stroke, starting at the opposite edge. Use a square to ensure your planed surface is square with the face and edge of your board, and go over it again with your plane if necessary.

JIGSAW

The jigsaw (Illus. 2-72 and 2-73) is a versatile tool which allows you to make straight or curved cuts. It can replace the band saw in most applications, although the band saw has a much larger maximum-cutting thickness. One advantage the jigsaw has is the ability to start a cut from the middle of a board. This allows you to cut large holes or cutouts. By using the correct blade, you can cut material up to 2 inches thick and make curves with radiuses as small as $\frac{1}{2}$ inch.

Jigsaws are usually sold either as regular or scrolling types. The scroller type has a cutter that can rotate, allowing a cut that isn't in line with the body of the saw. This allows slightly easier cutting of complicated curves. Instead of having to guide the entire saw through a series of changing curvatures, you simply push the blade along the line of cut

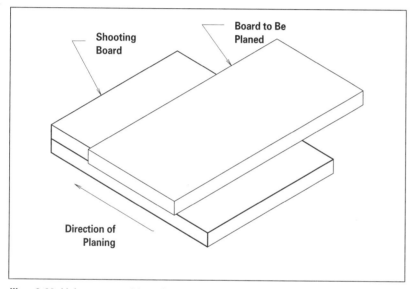

Illus. 2-69. Using a smoothing plane to plane end grain on a board.

Illus. 2-72. A typical scrolling jigsaw.

Illus. 2-70. Planing end grain with a block plane.

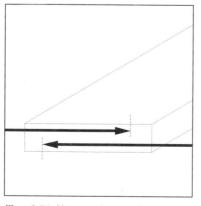

Illus. 2-71. How to plane end grain.

Illus. 2-73. A typical nonscrolling jigsaw.

Inside the shooting board illustration:

Shooting Board

Board to Be Planed

Direction of Planing

and it will rotate in the correct direction. While an advantage, this isn't a necessity. The more expensive models have this feature.

As with electric drills, variable speed (measured in strokes per minute) is an important feature in jigsaws. This allows you to match the speed of the blade's cutting action with both the hardness of the wood you are cutting and the type of blade you are using, which would be either a slow, smooth-cutting blade or a fast, rough-cutting blade. The speed control is usually built into the trigger switch (Illus. 2-74). Some models also having a locking mechanism and a speed limiter, which allow you to set the trigger to a particular speed instead of maintaining constant pressure on the trigger switch.

One of the biggest differences between lower- and higher-priced jigsaws is the size of the motors and the type of bearings, although the general construction and features offered are also factors. Lower-priced models typically have sleeve bearings instead of ball bearings. If you plan on using your jigsaw constantly, this may be a factor to consider, since

ball bearings would be preferable for a longer life. Otherwise, sleeve bearings will be just fine. The motor size, measured in amps or watts, is a measurement of how powerful the saw is. This can affect not only the speed of cuts in hard or thick material, but also the life of the motor. Pushing a small jigsaw through hard, thick wood is a sure way to shorten its life; a larger jigsaw (Illus. 2-75) is better suited to tougher work.

If your jigsaw doesn't come with a guide fence for making straight cuts, you can often get along without it by using a straight piece of 1 x 2 clamped to the board you are cutting. The guide fence will be useful, however, if you end up cutting out large circles, since most guide fences allow you to remove the fence from the guide and use the end of the guide as a pivot. Another feature you should look for in your jigsaw is a tilting sole plate, which will allow you to cut bevels with your jigsaw.

Using Your Jigsaw

The best way to achieve a good cut when using a jigsaw is to adjust your

cutting speed and feed rate. This may take practice. If you keep an eye on how your cut is proceeding, you will quickly learn when you are cutting too fast.

Jigsaw blades cut on the upstroke, which helps to keep the jigsaw against the work. This means the good side of your board should be facing down when it is being cut, to reduce splintering. Because of this, you have to make your layout marks on the reverse side. Keep this in mind when making your projects.

Jigsaw Blades

A wide range of blades are available for the jigsaw. Each one is designed for a particular job. Your blade selection will be important for the best possible results. Avoid general-purpose blades; pick the right one for the specific job, and keep spares handy in case of breakage.

When buying blades, be sure to purchase high-quality blades designed for use with wood. The extra cost of high-quality blades is minimal compared to the cost of your wood and other tools, so don't skimp. Higher-quality blades will have an obvious impact on your work.

You will have to decide whether to buy a set of blades or buy them individually. A set represents a savings in money when you factor in the cost of each individual blade. However, a set often includes metal-cutting blades or other blade styles that you won't use. Be aware that some brands of jigsaws require blades specially designed to fit them. If in doubt, ask at the store or bring in a sample when buying blades.

Jigsaw blades are available with different types of teeth (Illus. 2-77).

Illus. 2-74. A close-up of the trigger on a variable-speed jigsaw.

Illus. 2-75. This larger jigsaw is suited for professional work.

Utility blades (Illus. 2-78) have teeth that are literally punched out from the carbon-steel blade blanks; then each alternating tooth is bent slightly to each side, providing the "set" to the teeth. More expensive and smoother-cutting blades (Illus. 2-79) are hollow-ground from a better steel. The hollow-ground blades will produce better results, with less splintering and a much smoother surface.

In addition to the blade type, the smoothness of a cut is directly related to the number of teeth per inch (tpi) on the blade. The greater the number of teeth, the smoother the cut; however, the cutting speed will also be slower. Generally, a higher jigsaw speed and slower feed rate into the wood are required with fine-tooth blades.

When using your jigsaw, remember that the blades are thin and will bend or twist easily if you force them. When cutting, feed the jigsaw into the wood just fast enough to cut and not so fast that you are putting excessive pressure on the blade. Too much pressure may produce a cut that isn't perpendicular to the face of the board.

There are several specialty blades that can be useful (Illus. 2-80). A *scroll jigsaw blade* is a thin, narrow blade that allows you to cut very tight curves. A *long jigsaw blade* is designed to cut through stock that is too thick to be cut with a normal blade. *Laminate-cutting jigsaw blades* are hollow-ground with a large number of teeth that are reversed to cut on the down-stroke. This helps to prevent splintering the laminate surface if you are cutting with the laminate on top. Because the blade will push the jigsaw up and off the surface you are cutting, your feed rate should be slower than normal. The cutting edge of a *flush-cutting blade* extends well beyond the shank of the blade, to allow cutting flush against a vertical surface.

MEASUREMENT TOOLS

Ruler

A good 12-inch steel ruler with fine

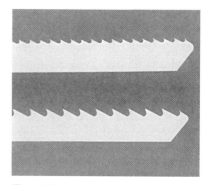
Illus. 2-78. A close-up of smooth and rough-cutting jigsaw utility blades.

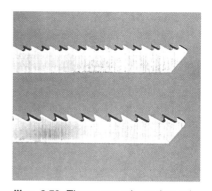
Illus. 2-79. These smooth- and rough-cutting jigsaw blades have high-quality hollow-ground teeth.

Illus. 2-76. Jigsaw blades with different types of ends for, from left to right, Bosch, universal and Makita, jigsaws.

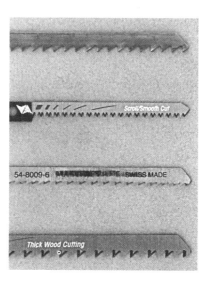
Illus. 2-77. Jigsaw blades are available with different types of teeth.

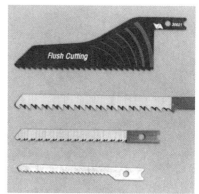
Illus. 2-80. Various special-purpose jigsaw blades. From top to bottom, they are flush-cutting, long, laminate-cutting, and scroll blades.

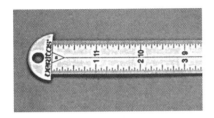

Illus. 2-81. A hook ruler.

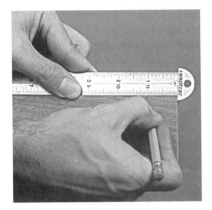

Illus. 2-82. Marking a board using a hook ruler.

graduations in imperial and metric dimensions is much more accurate than a tape measure for smaller measurements, such as the thickness and width of single boards. Buy one with easy-to-read divisions that start right at the end of the ruler. This allows you to measure from a definitive surface.

The hook ruler (Illus. 2-81 and 2-82) is a specialized ruler with a projection at the end that enables you to take accurate width or thickness measurements without being concerned about whether you properly aligned the edge of the ruler.

Tape Measure

Tape measures (Illus. 2-83 and 2-84) are needed for long measurements, such as marking a board when cutting it to length. They are available in several lengths. However, the shorter, 12-foot-long tape measures are ideal for woodworking because they

are easy to handle and are long enough. The graduations should be clearly marked and show $\frac{1}{16}$- or $\frac{1}{32}$-inch (1-mm) increments. Tape measures are available in imperial, metric, or combined imperial/metric versions. When selecting a tape measure, buy one with a wide tape and a locking feature that allows you to extend the tape and lock it in place.

Square

The square is one of the most important measuring tools for ensuring accurate, square cuts in handwork. Different types of square are available. They include try, framing, and combination squares. The *framing square* is a large, flat, L-shaped piece of metal with a wide tongue about 24 inches long and a narrower tongue measuring about 18 inches long (Illus. 2-85). It is graduated on all sides, and is excellent for truing up projects or marking a cutoff line on a

Illus. 2-83. A typical measuring tape.

Illus. 2-84. A close-up of the hook end of a measuring tape.

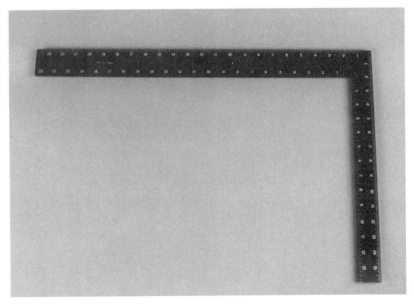

Illus. 2-85. A framing square.

wide board when the try square isn't long enough. The *try square* (Illus. 2-86) is much smaller, usually with an 8- or 12-inch tongue and a wooden, plastic, or metal body. Some versions aren't even graduated on their tongue, and are used for marking or verifying 90-degree angles only. Generally, they are used to mark a perfectly square line across the wood for cutting or to verify that the edge of the board is square to the face (Illus. 2-87). The *combination square* (Illus. 2-88) is a two-piece square with what is essentially a 12-inch ruler and a sliding head. The sliding head has both 45- and 90-degree fixed angles, allowing you to mark accurate square cuts. In addition, because of its sliding head the com-

Illus. 2-86. A try square.

Illus. 2-87. Marking a board for cross-cutting with a square. Note the angle of the pencil.

bination square can be used as a depth gauge and as a marking gauge. It can also be used exactly the same as a try square.

Measuring and Cutting Techniques

Both the tools and techniques used to measure can have an impact on how well the parts of any wood-working project fit together. It is important to use measuring tools to their best potential and to be aware of the limitation of their accuracy.

A measuring tape is only as accurate as its hook end. The end is designed to give an accurate reading both for inside and outside dimensions. This is accomplished by allowing the tang to shift by its own thickness, depending on what you are measuring. Since most measuring will be done to an outside dimension, such as when you are marking the length of a board for cutting, it is important to make sure your measuring tape will do this accurately.

To adjust your tape measure, first use a steel ruler to make a mark 12 inches from the end of a board. Next, use your measuring tape to measure this mark, and compare its reading. Bend the tang in or out slightly, depending on the reading, until the one-foot mark matches the mark on the board. Do this periodically to verify its accuracy.

There is also a common problem

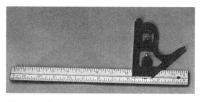

Illus. 2-88. A combination square.

involved in measuring accurately with a square. Once you have measured for the length of a piece, you have to draw a line straight across the board and perfectly perpendicular to the edge. This line acts as a guide for your saw. If the square isn't perfectly square, this will cause problems right from the start.

The best way to check a square is to lay its body against the edge of a board with its tongue on top of the board, perpendicular with the edge. Use a sharp pencil or knife to mark a line against the tongue, and then flip the square over so its body is on the same edge as before, pointing in the other direction. If its tongue doesn't line up with the line you previously made, the square isn't square.

It is almost impossible to be completely accurate when measuring and cutting by hand. This may not be a problem as long as you take it into consideration while building your project. If one measurement is dependent on the size of another piece, measure the first piece after it has been cut, and, if it deviates from the plans, you may be able to adjust the second measurement. If it is too long, you can also trim it down to size by recutting or using a hand plane.

When there are matching pieces, it may be important for them both to be the same size. In this case, the simple solution is to cut them together. This applies for drilling holes as well, where it may be easier to drill through two pieces of wood to get exactly matching holes than to measure and drill each one independently.

Whenever possible, you should use a common reference point for measurements, to avoid cumulative errors when measuring. For instance, if you were drilling 15 equally spaced holes into a board, a slight error in the measurement between each one will add up, and could mean that the last hole is off by quite a bit. If you measured for each hole from a common reference point, such as the end of the board, the last hole won't be any farther off than the accuracy of that single measurement (Illus. 2-89).

When marking your measurement for sawing or drilling, use a very sharp pencil or even a pointed knife. This will help to avoid the problems with fat lines, where you may forget which side of the line to cut on. When marking a line against a square, be sure to angle the pencil or knife so that the line you draw is exactly along the edge of the tongue on the marking gauge.

Whenever you build a project from plans, you must realize that all the measurements given are ideal, and often depend on each piece being exactly the size indicated, whether you measured and cut it yourself or you are using a standard thickness or width from your supplier. Therefore, you may occasionally need to adjust the measure- ments or even cut some of the final pieces to fit. To do this, test-assemble the pieces you have and measure for the last piece directly from the project.

CLAMPS

Clamps are essential. They are needed to hold pieces together while glue dries, to align parts while you drill or screw parts together, and to hold work on your bench while you saw or drill.

Many different types of clamp are available, of which the F-clamp is the most versatile for general work. For wider panels, the bar clamp is required. A basic set of clamps should include a pair of 12-inch F-clamps and a pair of 4-inch F-clamps (Illus. 2-90). The addition of three bar clamps will also be useful. C-clamps are of limited use, and, in any case, can be substituted for by a small F-clamp.

Clamps are available in a wide price range, so shop around to get the best value. Cheap clamps may

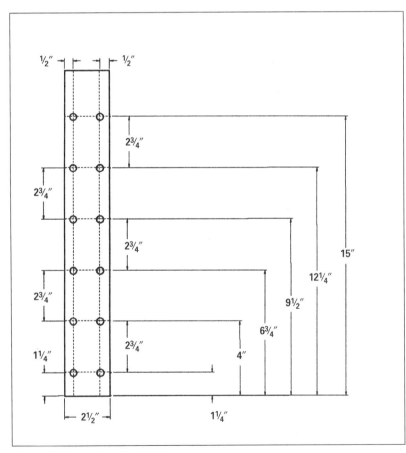

Illus. 2-89. Measuring multiple holes.

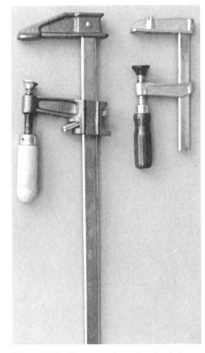

Illus. 2-90. Four- and twelve-inch-long F-clamps.

not be as durable or easy to work with; however, they will do the job. In addition, there are a few shop-made alternatives, which are discussed on pages 30 and 31.

The F-clamp comes in various sizes ranging in clamping capacity from 4 to 36 inches (Illus. 2-91 and 2-92). The size of the throats on F-clamps also varies. This size represents the maximum distance from the edge of the work that the clamp can reach to apply pressure. The F-clamp provides a positive, tight clamping action when you set the clamp head up against the wood and turn the clamp's handle. One model, the Quick Grip, provides for one-handed operation and can be tightened when you squeeze the handle rather than turning it like a screw.

When using the F-clamp to clamp over a long surface, you can use a wooden caul, which is simply a 2 x 2 piece of hardwood. This is placed over the wood before the clamp is applied, and will help apply an even pressure over the entire surface. This is especially useful where you aren't able to get a clamp in the center of a piece. It will also protect your project from marks

made by the clamps. If you don't use a caul, a thin scrap of wood no harder than your project's wood can be used to protect its surface.

Bar clamps come in a variety of types (Illus. 2-93), the most common requiring a $\frac{1}{2}$- or $\frac{3}{4}$-inch pipe. Others use a rectangular piece of steel or even a 2 x 4 or a narrow board as the bar. The clamps themselves have a tail and a head, infinitely adjustable for width depending on the length of the bar used. This type of clamp is typically used for gluing up wide panels or for final assembly of large projects.

Specialty clamps include those designed for mitered joints (Illus. 2-94), butt joints, and for holding on solid-wood edging while the glue dries (Illus. 2-95). These specialty clamps can be purchased as required.

Alternatives to Clamps

While clamps are almost essential for woodworking, there are some inexpensive alternatives. Although these alternatives won't provide the same clamping pressure as commercial clamps do, in most cases the clamp-

ing pressure will be adequate. In addition, these methods won't be as convenient—possibly lengthening the time it takes to make your project while you wait for each section to

Illus. 2-92. F-clamps at work.

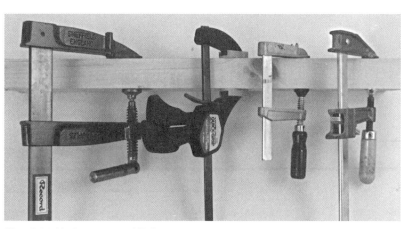

Illus. 2-91. Various types of F-clamp.

Illus. 2-93. Various types of bar clamp.

dry. Saving time is one reason professional woodworking shops have a multitude of clamps available.

One alternative is a commercial workbench. The Black & Decker Workmate (Illus. 2-96) has a built-in vise and dog-holes in its top, which can also be used for clamping. You can also make a basic bar clamp from a few 2 x 4s with round dog-holes drilled along its length (Illus. 2-97). Use steel or wooden dogs to fit the holes (Illus. 2-98), and spacers from scrap wood and wedges to provide the clamping pressure.

Even if your workbench doesn't have a vise, it can serve for clamping if it has dog-holes. You can make spacers and wedges to use on your workbench (Illus. 2-99 and 2-100).

Strong tape can be wrapped around the parts of small projects (Illus. 2-101).

Illus. 2-96. This worktable can be used for clamping.

Illus. 2-97. This shop-made bar clamp consists of 2 x 4 lumber, wooden bench dogs, and wedges.

Illus. 2-94. A miter clamp.

Illus. 2-95. Two different sizes of spring clamps.

HELPFUL TOOLS AND ACCESSORIES

Power Sanders

A power sander (Illus. 2-102) is basically a very efficient labor-saving tool. While you can do all the sanding you will ever need by hand, you may soon find out how much time and effort it takes, especially to do a good job on a large project. Power sanders are available that will allow you to do a better job of sanding with very little effort, and much less time.

Power sanders do kick up quite a bit of sawdust. Some models are available with dust collectors (Illus. 2-103). However, don't expect them to eliminate the sawdust. If at all possible, use a power sander outdoors. They also make a fair bit of noise due to their rapid vibrating action.

As a simple alternative to handsanding, the *finishing sander* is a good choice. The $^1/_4$-sheet sanders (Illus. 2-104) will suit most needs, are easy to handle, and are very inexpensive to operate, because they use standard sheets of sandpaper. The sandpaper is moved in fixed orbits of 11,000 to 15,000 orbits per minute, and the orbits range in

Illus. 2-98. Brass bench dogs and a dog clamp.

diameter from $\frac{1}{16}$ to $\frac{1}{8}$ inch. The $\frac{1}{4}$-sheet model is easy to use, yet large enough for most projects.

If you expect to do a lot of woodworking, you may want to buy a *random-orbit sander* (Illus. 2-105) instead of a finishing sander. It combines the motion of the orbital sander with a random action, leaving a better surface. Random-orbit sanders are typically built with stronger motors than finishing sanders, making them more aggressive. The disadvantage is that random-orbit sanders are typically round, which makes it difficult for them to sand in corners. They also require special sanding discs, which are more expensive than sandpaper sheets, but generally last longer.

Illus. 2-102. A round palm sander.

Illus. 2-99. Shop-made bench dogs and wedges.

Illus. 2-101. Using tape to clamp the wood pieces together while gluing them up.

Illus. 2-103. A $\frac{1}{4}$-sheet finishing sander with a dust collector.

Illus. 2-100. Clamping with shop-made bench dogs and wedges on a workbench.

Illus. 2-104. A $\frac{1}{4}$-sheet finishing sander. Finishing sanders will prove helpful in most sanding operations, are easy to handle, and are inexpensive to operate.

Illus. 2-105. A random-orbit sander with a dust collector.

Using Your Power Sander With power sanders, it is important to use proper pressure and let the machine do the work. Use enough pressure to be in control of the tool, but don't apply excessive pressure. This may overload the motor, shortening its life. The extra pressure will also slow down your sanding.

Chisels

Eventually, you may find a need for a chisel (Illus. 2-106) in your workshop. It is useful for cleaning out waste wood or paring joints to size.

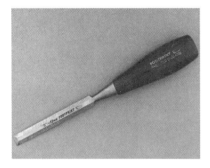

Illus. 2-106. A chisel can be used to make many hand-cut joints, to remove waste wood, or to pare joints to size.

With a chisel, you can make most hand-cut joints such as dovetails or mortise-and-tenon joints, as well as trim a lap joint for a perfect fit. Chisels come in various sizes, from $\frac{1}{4}$ inch and up. These sizes indicate the width of the blade. A bevel-edge chisel is the most versatile, allowing it to reach into tight spaces and corners. A mallet is often used with a chisel; however, in many cases you will only need to pare away the wood with firm hand pressure.

Portable Drill Guides

Portable drill guides are small-scale replacements for a drill press that you can use with your hand drill. While not as large and versatile as the drill press, they provide some of the benefits; for example, they can drill holes perfectly perpendicular to the surface to a specified depth.

Three basic types of drill guide

Illus. 2-107. A drill-press-type drill guide. You take your work to this drill guide.

are available. One is more like the traditional drill press, complete with a table (Illus. 2-107). Your drill clamps into the top, which is equipped with a rack-and-pinion mechanism, allowing you to lower the drill and drill bit into the wood placed on the table to a specified and controlled depth. Like full-size drill presses, there is a limit to the distance the hole can be drilled from the edge of your board, depending on the distance between the chuck and the guide bars. There is also a limit to the depth of hole that you can drill.

The second type of drill guide does not actually have a table (Illus. 2-108). The drill is held in a guide, which also allows you to drill holes perpendicular to or even at an angle to the surface. There is no table, so instead of taking the wood to the drill, you take the drill to the wood. With this type of drill guide, you can drill holes anywhere on the surface of the wood.

The last type is essentially a drill-bit guide rather than a drill guide (Illus. 2-109). With this device, you are strictly limited to twist or brad-point drills and to specific diameters

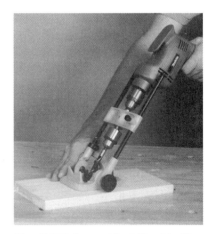

Illus. 2-108. A portable drill guide. You take this drill guide to your work.

that match the drill bushings; in this case, from $\frac{1}{4}$ to $\frac{1}{2}$ inch in diameter. Even so, it can be a cheap alternative to the first two drill guide types, and is especially handy for drilling into dowels.

Drill Level Stick-Ons

Drill level stick-ons have two or more levels that mount on your drill with sticky pads to provide you with some extra feedback when drilling (Illus. 2-110). While not as accurate as a drill guide, they are a great help when drilling freehand. When using a drill level stick-on, you can eventually develop your own sense of when the drill is straight, and rely on the drill level less and less. Two varieties are available, each one designed for a specific style of drill body.

Drilling Depth Stops

Depth stops (Illus. 2-111) are used with twist or brad-point drill bits. These collars are tightened onto the drill bit at the required depth and will prevent you from drilling too deep. These are indispensable when you are drilling dowel holes on the face of boards, since it is very easy to drill too deep and create a hole through your work. Individually sized collars or adjustable collars are available.

Chamfering Tool

A chamfering tool (Illus. 2-112) allows you to easily take the sharp edges off boards or the finished project. Chamfering tools are used instead of sandpaper or power sanders, and may give you uneven results. The version shown in Illus. 2-112 comes as a set of two, and cuts a $\frac{1}{16}$-, $\frac{1}{8}$-, $\frac{3}{16}$-, and $\frac{1}{4}$-inch radius. If you prefer a true chamfer rather than a radius, you can use your bench plane to knock off the corners (Illus. 2-113).

Mallet

You can use a waste scrap of wood and your hammer instead of a mallet, but a mallet (Illus. 2-114) will be more convenient. It is used to give some extra force to a chisel or force a dowel joint together. You should buy a flat-faced mallet; round mallets are primarily for woodcarving tools.

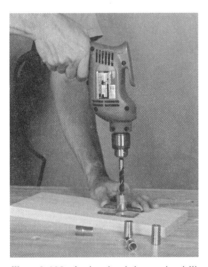

Illus. 2-109. A simple right-angle drill guide.

Illus. 2-111. Two types of drill-depth stop.

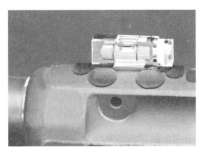

Illus. 2-110. A drill level stick-on.

Illus. 2-112. Using a radius/chamfering tool.

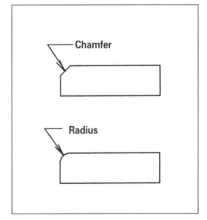

Illus. 2-113. Compare the chamfer to the radius.

KEEPING TOOLS SHARP

Dull tools will not only frustrate you by cutting slowly, they may also give you very poor results when they are being used. While no tool will stay sharp forever, if you treat all cutting edges with respect, you can help keep the edges sharp longer and avoid nicks in things like plane blades, which are difficult to correct. This means the following: using a guard over your handsaw blade; setting your plane on its side or retracting its blade when it is not in use; making sure there is no dust or sand on your wood before you begin cutting it; sanding only after you have done all your drilling and cutting; and being careful with your drill bits, to avoid having the cutting edge come in contact with any other metal.

If you are treating the cutting edges of your tools with respect and aren't using them regularly, they will stay sharp for quite a while. When they do become dull, you will need special sharpening stones, files, and accessories to properly sharpen them, or to repair any damage to their cutting surfaces. If you aren't prepared to buy the equipment and sharpen them yourself, you can have them professionally sharpened for a modest cost.

FASTENING MATERIALS AND TECHNIQUES

Woodworking projects, with the exception of those that are carved or turned, are constructed from several smaller parts that have to be joined together. Traditional craftsmanship would use dovetails, mortise-and-tenon joints, and similar joints that are designed for high strength without mechanical fasteners. While these techniques are fine for woodworkers who have the right tools or the time and patience to do them by hand, there are a number of much easier ways to construct projects. These are discussed below.

Nails

Nails are a good standby for simple, fast construction. They are especially good for outdoor projects. They are not as good as screws for pure holding power, and the only good way to hide a nail head is with wood filler, which always shows. Because they don't have much holding power, they shouldn't be used where the pieces joined will be subjected to high stress, such as a chair. Nails come in many sizes and styles, from $1/2$-inch brads to 4-inch spikes (Illus. 2-115–2-117).

One fundamental difference between two types of nails—finish-

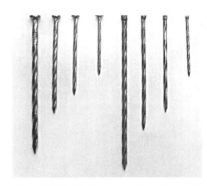

Illus. 2-116. Various lengths of spiral, flathead, and finishing nails.

Illus. 2-117. Specialty nails. The framing nail on the left can be easily removed. The ribbed nail shown on the right has increased holding power.

Illus. 2-114. A mallet is sometimes convenient for hitting a chisel with extra force or for forcing a dowel joint together.

Illus. 2-115. Various lengths of regular flathead and finishing nails.

ing and flathead nails—is their head. Finishing nails have small, compact heads that are meant to be set below the surface of the wood; the remaining hole is usually filled with wood filler. Flathead nails have flat heads which can't be easily hidden, yet these nails provide more strength than finishing nails because their heads resist being pulled through the wood if stress is applied.

For outdoor projects, it is important to use galvanized nails or other specially coated nails. Otherwise, you will soon be faced with rust stains on your project.

When nailing into softwood, no pilot holes are necessary unless you are nailing close to the end of a board, which will easily split unless a pilot hole is drilled. For hardwood, pilot holes are almost always needed not only to prevent splitting, but to ensure that you can hammer the nail in straight without bending it.

Screws

Screws are the strongest mechanical fastener you can use for wood. While properly made dovetail, mortise-and-tenon, or other similar joints are more than strong enough without mechanical fasteners, most simple construction techniques can benefit from screws.

Screws are available in a wide range of sizes and lengths, and in different head types (Illus. 2-118). Which screw you use will depend on the use and the thickness of the boards you are screwing together. While most wood joints are usually fastened with a #6 or #8 screw in lengths from $\frac{3}{8}$ to $1\frac{1}{4}$ inches (Illus. 2-119), longer screws may be needed for some projects.

Except for cut-brass screws,

which are almost always slotted, the two most prevalent driver-style screws in woodworking are the Phillips and Robertson (square-drive) screws (Illus. 2-120–2-122). They both allow you to apply enough torque, and won't allow the screwdriver to slip off as the slotted screw will—assuming the business end of your screwdriver is in good shape. In actual performance, however, the square-drive screw allows for more torque and almost no slipping.

Illus. 2-118. A variety of different screws. From left to right, they are a deck screw, a drywall screw, a cut brass screw, an ordinary woodworking screw, and a particleboard screw.

Illus. 2-119. Various lengths of #8 screws.

Unlike Phillips screws, excessive downward pressure is not needed to drive them, even at high torque. If you have a choice, use square-drive screws.

Flathead or panhead screws are most commonly used on hardware. Brass screws are a common choice for brass hardware. The packaging or catalogue information should

Illus. 2-120. Three different types of screw heads. From left to right, they are Robertson, Phillips, and slotted screws.

Illus. 2-121. A top view showing the heads on Robertson, Phillips, and slotted screws.

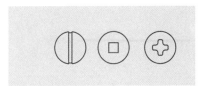

Illus. 2-122. Slotted, Robertson, and Phillips screws.

indicate the correct screw size to use.

The threads on woodworking screws (Illus. 2-123 and 2-124) can be either cut or rolled. The shank on screws with cut threads will have the same or a larger diameter than the threads themselves, requiring not only a pilot hole, but also a clearance hole. Rolled threads are larger in diameter than the shank. The shank is usually a standard size, such as $\frac{1}{8}$ inch, which lets you drill a pilot hole the same size as the shank yet still provides lots of material for the threads to grip.

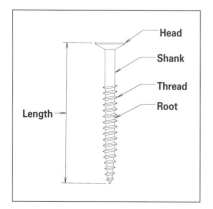

Illus. 2-123. The different parts of a screw.

Screws with cut threads are the most commonly available woodworking screws. Rolled threads are usually found on particleboard screws, which are also ideal for all-around woodworking construction. When working with particleboard, be sure to use particleboard screws, because they hold better than ordinary wood screws in the relatively soft particleboard material.

Be sure to use coated, galvanized or stainless-steel screws for outdoor projects to reduce the possibility of rust. Also, remember that screwing into end grain will give you a weaker joint than screwing into edge or face grain because the short grain presented to the screw threads by end grain will break away easily. Where great strength is important, you can use a dowel inserted into a hole drilled lengthwise through the end, just far enough for the screw to grab (Illus. 2-125).

Pilot Holes Drilling pilot holes for screws in hardwood is almost always required. In softwood such as poplar or pine, you may not need to drill a pilot hole, just the countersink

and counterbore holes. Many screw-hole formers are available that make the job easier (see pages 24 and 25); however, it is possible to make the pilot holes with drill bits and a countersink bit. The hole you drill will depend on the type of screw you are using and whether you intend to hide the screw head under a plug.

A pilot hole (Illus. 2-126) allows the screw to bore easily into the wood while leaving enough material around it for the screw threads to bite into. A *clearance hole* is needed when you are using woodworking screws with shanks the same diameter as the threads, or to provide thread clearance where you need to draw two pieces of wood tightly together. The *counterbore hole* allows the head of the screw to be hidden under the surface of the wood with a plug; the *countersink hole* provides the right angle for the base of the screw head to bear onto and leaves the top of a flathead screw flush with the wood surface.

If you use a commercial screw former, you can drill the clearance, counterbore, and countersink holes all at once (Illus. 2-127 and 2-128). If you are using drills and a countersink, you have to drill them one at a time.

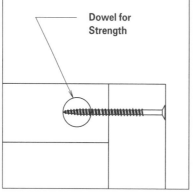

Illus. 2-125. A dowel provides extra strength in end-grain screwing.

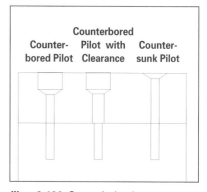

Illus. 2-126. Screw hole plugs.

Illus. 2-124. Screw head shapes.

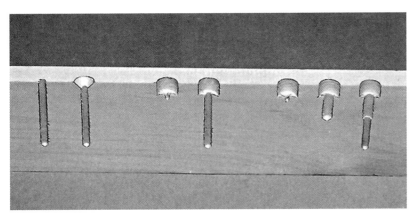

Illus. 2-127. The various steps required to make the pilot holes made with countersink and drill bits. From left to right, they are countersunk holes, counterbored holes, and counterbored holes with a clearance hole.

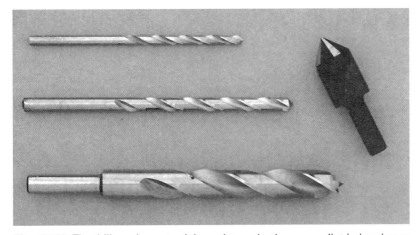

Illus. 2-128. The drills and countersink used to make the screw pilot holes shown in Illus. 2-127.

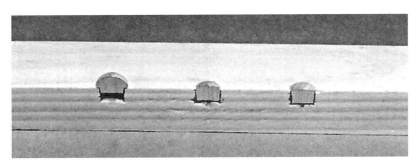

Illus. 2-129. Examples of screw-hole plugs. From left to right, they are button, rounded, and flush plugs.

To make a countersunk pilot hole, first drill the countersink and then drill the pilot hole, centered in the countersink hole.

To make a counterbored pilot hole, drill the counterbore first to a depth that will allow you to add a plug. Then drill the pilot hole, centered in the counterbore.

To make a counterbored pilot hole with a clearance hole, drill the counterbore first to a depth that will allow you to add a plug. Next, drill the clearance hole, centering it in the counterbore. Then drill the pilot hole centered in the clearance hole.

Screw-Hole Plugs When using screws for construction, you can use screw-hole plugs to hide the screw heads. They can be made to be virtually invisible, or added as a decorative element. Plugs come in three types: flush, rounded, or button (Illus. 2-129 and 2-130). In most cases, they are glued in place and will be permanent. However, if you want

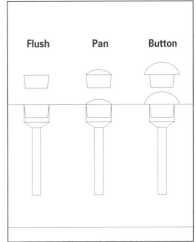

Illus. 2-130. Screw-hole plugs. From left to right, they are flush, rounded, and button plugs.

to be able to remove the screws at a later date, such as when using screws that will mount something on a wall, you can use button plugs that are simply pushed into place. Flush plugs are usually used to hide the screw hole, while rounded and button plugs are often used to add a decorative feature. While the plugs are almost always sold in a light-colored hardwood such as birch, it is possible to get them in oak or cherry. You may even want to stain or paint the plugs a contrasting color before they are installed.

Rounded and button plugs are added after sanding is complete. The flush plugs should be installed before you start the sanding. Apply glue and tap them in place so they are as flush as possible with the surrounding wood; allow them to dry before sanding.

3
MAKING JOINTS

Joints are a fundamental part of woodworking; you can't make much without them. A wide array of joints are possible, many requiring special equipment or a great deal of time and skill to use properly. For our purposes, we will focus on a few joints that are strong and easy to make with a limited number of tools and a modest amount of time.

The strength of the joint is a critical factor for most projects and will influence the useful life of your project. Poorly made joints not only look bad, they aren't likely to last very long, and will either ruin the project or eventually need repairs.

Joints that take a lot of stress, like those in a chair, require special consideration during the design and construction of the project. The following joints represent a good cross section of all the joints needed to build the projects in this book. However, they each have specific functions and limitations.

GLUING JOINTS

Glue is seldom used by itself to fasten joints that will be experiencing great stress, unless the joint itself provides a good mechanical lock, such as dovetails or mortise-and-tenon joints. For the projects in this book, glue will usually be used with dowels or nails or screws, except in specific situations.

Glue, if properly applied under certain conditions, will create a joint that is stronger than the wood itself. This only occurs when face grain is glued to face grain, such as when edge-gluing boards or gluing two boards together to create a thicker board. End-grain gluing is very weak and is always backed up with a mechanical fasteners such as screws or dowels. This is due to the nature of wood; end grain will suck away much of the glue, and will not provide much grip between the parts of the joint.

Always use a good-quality glue. While white glue is traditionally used for wood, the yellow versions are more suitable, since they have a higher viscosity and higher strength as well as shorter drying times. If you have a selection of glue, use white or yellow glues for light-colored woods and the light brown glue for darker wood to reduce the visibility of glue lines. Water-resistant and waterproof glues are also available for special applications.

Apply glue to both mating surfaces in a thin layer, first applying a bead (Illus. 3-1), and then spreading it (Illus. 3-2) with a stick or your finger. This will help prevent dry spots when the two pieces are joined together. Be sure to apply just enough glue so you don't end up with lots of squeeze-out. This is something that you will be able to judge with practice. If lots of glue is squeezed out, be sure to remove it right away so it doesn't harden on the surface of your wood and become difficult to remove, or soak into the wood and affect your finish.

Glued joints should be clamped with clamps, screws, or by other means. In some cases, clamping won't be needed, such as when you are simply gluing on a decorative molding or

Illus. 3-1. Applying a bead of glue to a mating surface.

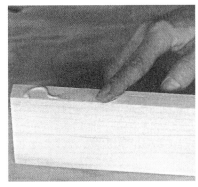
Illus. 3-2. Spread the glue with your finger or a stick.

something similar. Ideally, a very small bead of squeeze-out should appear after clamping, indicating that there was enough glue for the joint.

Clamping pressure should be tight, but not excessive. If it's excessive, you risk starving the joint of glue. Ordinarily, you should not be able to see a thick glue joint.

MITER JOINTS

A miter joint is a joint formed with an angle. The most common example of a miter joint is in a picture frame, where each piece is cut on a 45-degree angle and the pieces then joined together. These types of joint are not meant to be strong by themselves, and require nails, screws, or dowels to strengthen them.

Miter joints are either face- or edge-joined (see Illus. 2-63). Face joints are used on picture frames. An edge miter can be used to make a box where the end grain won't show at the corners.

Miters can be cut freehand with a saw or in a miter box. If you cut them freehand, trimming them with a block plane will probably be necessary to get a tight, accurate fit. The

miter box will provide a much better cut, but the miters may still need to be trimmed with a block plane.

When using a miter box, simply place the wood in the box and your saw will be guided at a 45-degree angle by the miter box's sides. Even though you are using a miter box, you still need to make sure that your saw strokes are smooth, even, and straight. With standard miter boxes, gradual wear of the guide slots may make your miters inaccurate over time. When this happens, it's time to get a new miter box.

When cutting a tall face miter or wide edge miter, you will have to cut it by hand. Either use a square to mark the 45-degree angle or draw

reference lines as shown in Illus. 3-3. Then cut to the outside of the line, being very careful to saw with smooth, even strokes, and keeping the blade as straight as possible.

When reinforcing miter joints (Illus. 3-4), be sure to glue and clamp the joint first. If using nails, first drill a pilot hole diagonally through the joint to ensure that your nails start at the correct angle; then hammer the nails in. The pilot hole will also ensure you don't split the wood. Screws are a stronger alternative, and also require pilot holes.

Dowels, unlike nails or screws, don't have to show. They do require carefully lined-up dowel holes, which must be made before the joint

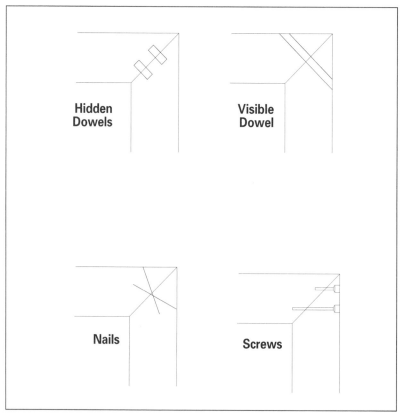

Illus. 3-4. Reinforcing a miter cut with nails, dowels, or screws.

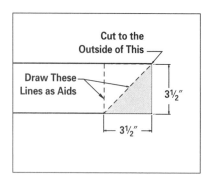

Illus. 3-3. Marking reference lines for hand-cutting a miter.

is glued. An alternate method is to drill a hole all the way through the joint after it has been glued and clamped, and then insert a long dowel all the way through, cutting off the excess dowel at the surface of the wood. This provides for a strong joint with a decorative element. Be sure to use a standard dowel for this, not a fluted one.

LAP JOINTS

The three varieties of lap joints—the corner, T-shaped, and cross-lap joints (Illus. 3-5–3-8)—are used when frame members are joined together. They are strong, easy-to-make joints that are useful where right-angle construction of flat boards is required. The corner lap joint is the only one used for the projects in this book. It is very useful where a butt joint won't provide enough strength or if you don't want to see screw or nail holes.

The corner lap joint can be cut solely with a handsaw or backsaw. A chisel is a handy accessory for this type of joint, allowing you to smoothen or adjust the joint after cutting it. For the T-shaped and cross-lap joints, a chisel is necessary, because it isn't possible to complete-ly saw out the waste.

Lap joints can also be used as an alternative to the edge miter joint. The lap joint provides a large surface for gluing, which makes it a very strong joint that doesn't require mechanical fasteners.

To make a corner lap joint, use the pieces themselves to mark the length of the joint. Lay the piece you are working on first down on your work surface. Lay the second piece on top so that its edge is flush with the end of the first piece. Use a sharp pencil or knife to mark the width of the lap joint, using the inside edge of the top piece as a guide. Next, use a square to make a perpendicular mark along both edges so that they meet the line you drew on the face. Then measure the thickness of the board, calculate half this thickness, and mark this depth on both sides and at the end. Join the marks with a straight-edge so that you have framed the area which will be cut out.

Using a handsaw (a backsaw is recommended), cut to the inside of the lines, starting with the shoulder of the lap joint. Once this is cut, saw out the cheek so that your cut meets up with the shoulder cut to remove the waste piece. Repeat the process with the second part, this time using the first lap to establish the thickness of the second lap. This will make it easier to keep the boards flush, once joined. If possible, trim the surfaces with a sharp chisel, or even a sand-ing block.

When cutting the lap joint, you may want to leave the cheek a little longer than necessary; you can always sand the excess off or trim it with a plane after the joint is glued and dry. To glue the lap joints, you have to clamp the two faces together. Make sure the joint is square and its

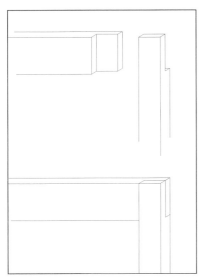

Illus. 3-5. A corner lap joint.

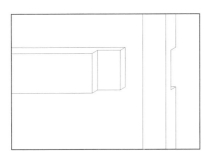

Illus. 3-6. A T-shaped lap joint.

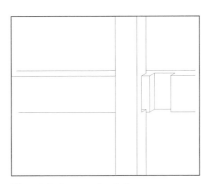

Illus. 3-7. A cross-lap joint.

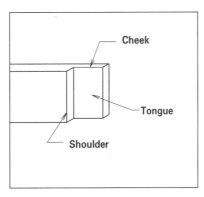

Illus. 3-8. Anatomy of a lap joint.

cheeks are tight against one another before leaving it to dry.

BUTT JOINTS

Butt joints are the simplest joints to make, and are the ideal joint in most applications, especially for box-type construction. In virtually all cases, the joint must be reinforced with nails, screws, or dowels, but is quite strong once this is done. As the name implies, two pieces of wood are butted together, to produce an edge, case, or frame joint (Illus. 3-9–3-11). Making them is as simple as cutting out two pieces of wood with straight, even ends and edges. Line up the pieces so that they are flush and clamp them in place. To ensure a square cut, you can use a miter box and trim the cut with a block plane. It is important that the pieces be perfectly square, or your joint will also end up out of square.

A butt joint can be reinforced either with blind dowels that can't be seen once the joint is glued, or with visible dowels (Illus. 3-12). For visible dowels, drill a hole through the joined pieces and glue a standard dowel in place. Cut and trim off the end of the dowel, or let it extend past the surface by $\frac{1}{8}$ inch or less and bevel its edge with sandpaper for a decorative look. Use dowels of contrasting color, or stain them beforehand for a unique touch.

When reinforcing a butt joint with nails, drill a pilot hole slightly smaller than the nail diameter to avoid splitting the wood. For screws, use counterbored piloted screw holes for the same reason. If you are using screws or nails to reinforce the joint, you won't have to clamp the joint while the glue dries.

DOWELS

If you want to make strong joints where the mechanical fastener doesn't show, you can't beat the dowel joint for simplicity (Illus. 3-12). Lining up the dowel holes is the biggest challenge when making a good dowel joint; however, there are several methods and inexpensive accessories available to help out.

Dowels can be plain or fluted. If the end of your dowel will show, then a plain one should be used. For hidden dowels, the fluted dowel is better, since it allows the glue to squeeze out of the hole and around the dowel, giving a better bond with the wood and improving its strength. Another useful feature is chamfered edges. This helps with insertion, and enables more glue to flow up the side of the dowel, instead of being pushed to the bottom of the dowel hole.

Doweling Guides

If you expect to use dowels for your projects, a dowel guide (Illus. 3-13) is a useful aid for drilling accurate, matching dowel holes. Most drill guides accommodate two or three sizes of dowels, the standard dowels being $\frac{1}{4}$, $\frac{3}{8}$, and $\frac{1}{2}$ inch in diameter. The guide allows you to align your

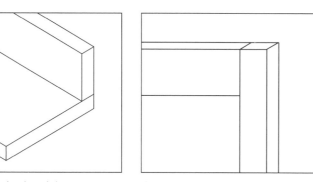

Illus. 3-9. An edge butt joint.

Illus. 3-11. A frame butt joint.

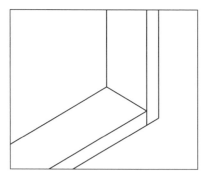

Illus. 3-10. A case butt joint.

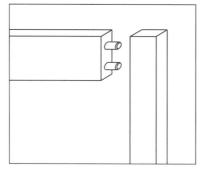

Illus. 3-12. A frame butt joint reinforced with dowels.

dowels both from the edge of the boards to ensure a flush joint, and laterally to ensure all your dowels will line up. The guide is especially useful for butt joints and for lining up boards when edge-gluing. It cannot be used for dowels that must be drilled more than a couple of inches in from the edge of your board.

Doweling Centers

Dowel centers (Illus. 3-14) allow you to drill dowel holes in the first piece, and easily align the matching dowel's holes into the second piece of your joint. These are used in place of a dowel jig, and are an inexpensive alternative, although they are not as easy to use. Simply drill your first dowel holes, place the centers in the holes, align the mating parts, and press them into the centers. The centers will mark the exact center for drilling the matching dowel holes.

Marking for Dowel Joints

The key to successful dowel joints is to mark and drill the holes accurately, especially if you aren't using a dowel guide or centers (Illus. 3-15). Decide on a reference face and edge for each joint, and measure from these references on both pieces to ensure that the edges and/or face will be flush after the joint is put together.

GLUING UP BOARDS

When a project requires boards that are wider than commonly available ones, you will have to glue two or more standard-size boards together. Although you can buy glued-up panels from some outlets, you will be paying a premium, and you might not get a perfect match between the glued-up panels you buy and the rest of the wood you use in the project. Sometimes this won't matter; however, if it does, then your best option is to make the glued-up panel yourself.

To make your own glued-up panel, you need to make sure that the edges of each board are square before gluing them together. Check the edges first with your square; if

they aren't exactly square to the face, try another board. Another way to check is to test-fit your boards. Lay them down on your work surface and place their edges together. If you see any gaps, try another board or change the orientation of the boards, which works especially well if you are gluing up pieces that were cut from the same board. In this case, if the edges aren't quite square, flip one piece over; the errors will cancel each other out, making a perfect match and a tight joint.

If the edges aren't square, or have defects that don't allow a clean joint between the boards, you can use a hand plane to correct the problem. Position each set of two boards flat on your workbench as they would be if you were gluing them together, and then "fold" them like a book so the edges to be glued are together and facing up. Clamp the boards or hold them in a vise and plane the edges of both boards together, taking

Illus. 3-13. Using a doweling jig to drill holes for dowels.

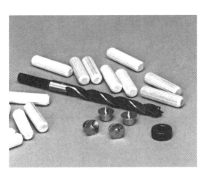

Illus. 3-14. A doweling kit with dowels, drill bit, depth stop, and dowel centers.

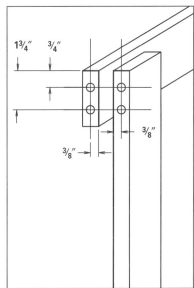

Illus. 3-15. Marking drill holes for a dowel joint.

very fine shavings. Not only does this give you a wider surface to plane on, but also if you don't plane the edge perfectly square, the inaccuracy will cancel itself out when the two surfaces are glued together.

At the same time, you should be paying attention to how the boards will look when they are glued together. If they have knots, lighter or darker streaks, or a particular grain pattern, then you may want the boards to be oriented in a certain way either to minimize or to accentuate these characteristics, depending on your personal preference.

To glue up the panel, apply glue to both edges and spread it with your finger so that you have a thin, even coating before pressing the pieces together. Keep track of which side of the glued-up panel will be visible in your project, and make certain that the joint on this side is perfectly flush. Also, if you have already cut your pieces to length, make sure that the ends are flush. In some cases, it may be easier to glue up the panel with pieces a couple of inches longer than the final size and cut the panel to length after it is dry.

To clamp the pieces together, you can use a set of bar clamps, F-clamps, or even bench dogs on your workbench. If using bar or F-clamps, you should have clamps on both sides of the wood, such as two on the underside of the wood near each end and one on top in the middle; this helps prevent cupping of the panel while it is drying.

In some cases, you may not have to clamp the boards together, or you may not have the clamps you need. If the joint between the boards is even and doesn't have any spaces between the edges, you can use another technique. Spread the glue on both edges as before, but wait until the glue is tacky before pressing the pieces together. This technique will work on short boards. When gluing up long boards, use clamps.

4
WOOD SELECTION

The most important part of any woodworking project is the wood. Knowing how to select and buy this material and knowing its working characteristics are key components in building a successful project.

You may have a plentiful or a limited supply of wood available where you live, depending on which species grow in your area. If you are able to purchase exotic woods, then prices will reflect the shipping and handling costs. It is not important that you use the exact species recommended for the project, as long as the wood you use has the same properties.

When deciding on which wood to use, consider the project's design and intended use, and whether the wood's properties will help serve these purposes. The strength of the wood can be very important. For example, a chair should be built with a hard wood that will enable the joints to withstand the constant stress that's placed on it, while a night table or drawer can easily be made with a softer wood. Softer woods are economical and easy to work, yet aren't as strong, tough, or durable as the harder varieties of wood.

When selecting boards with the properties you want, remember that the terms hardwood and softwood don't refer to the hardness of the wood. Poplar, which is classified as a hardwood, is very similar to pine in hardness and strength, even though pine is a softwood. The term hardwood refers to deciduous trees, which have leaves that shed seasonally. Softwood refers to coniferous trees, commonly known as evergreens.

The color and grain of the wood are other characteristics which can add further interest to your projects. The color of the wood is dependent on its species, although there is some variation in color between individual trees. There is a significant difference in color between the heartwood and sapwood in the same species of wood. *Heartwood* is the interior of the tree, which no longer carries sap. The *sapwood* is the outer layer of the tree just under the bark, which is still living. The relative widths of these two layers also varies between species. If your boards have two tones of color caused by the heartwood and sapwood, either avoid using them or select them specifically to add some interest to the project, depending on your taste.

Grain is related to the orientation of the annual rings of the tree and how they appear in the dressed wood (Illus. 4-1). The contrasting colors common in oak make a very distinct grain pattern, while the relative uniformity of pine or poplar's annual rings makes a very plain grain.

The orientation of the annual rings in the board (i.e., how the board is cut from the tree) affects the look of the grain. If you are able to pick through your wood source, look for boards that appeal to you. If making a larger project that requires several boards, be sure to select boards which come closest to each other in appearance.

LUMBER GRADING

The grade of your lumber can have a great impact on both its cost and the amount of usable wood you actually get. There are many grades of lumber, usually relating to how few knots and other blemishes are present and the minimum length and width of the totally clear pieces available after the blemishes are cut out of the board. Since most of the projects in this book use standard-width boards (Tables 4-1 and 4-2), you should keep this in mind when selecting your lumber.

Naturally, the better the grade, the more you will pay for your lumber. If you are making a project with small

Illus. 4-1. Various sizes and species of dressed lumber.

pieces, a lower grade may yield all the clear pieces you need at a lower cost. For larger projects where you want knot- and blemish-free wood, use a higher grade. Some higher-quality grades are only applied to one side of the board. The second side will be of a lesser grade. If only one side of the board will show, you may want to consider this option.

Lumberyards in most localities can legally define their own grading systems. Most, however, grade their lumber according to local or national association standards. It is important to know whether you want blemish-free wood or wood with character before you go shopping.

The best method of selecting lumber is to get the pricing for the grades your lumberyard carries and visually inspect the lumber before deciding on whether it is suitable. If you buy your lumber from a retail building center, you may have very little choice in the grades available.

LUMBER MEASUREMENTS

Lumber is measured in two ways. Nominal measurements (Illus. 4-2 and 4-3) are for rough green lumber after it has been cut at the sawmill. The price you pay is usually based on this measurement. However, once the wood is dressed, its final (usable) dimensions will be less. For example, a 1 x 6-inch x 8-foot nominal board will typically be $\frac{3}{4}$ x $5\frac{1}{2}$ inches x 8 feet once it is surfaced (dressed) on all four sides (Table 4-3). It is very

important to take this into account when calculating the wood you require. Usually, the lumberyard will dress wood to any size you want (sometimes at a charge, depending on your specifications). However,

Illus. 4-3. Rough and dressed boards, not cut from the same board.

Nominal Width (Inches)	Standard Width (Inches)	Standard Width (Millimeters)
2	$1\frac{1}{2}$	38 mm
3	$2\frac{1}{2}$	64 mm
4	$3\frac{1}{2}$	89 mm
5	$4\frac{1}{2}$	114 mm
6	$5\frac{1}{2}$	140 mm
8	$7\frac{1}{4}$	184 mm
10	$9\frac{1}{4}$	235 mm
12	$11\frac{1}{4}$	286 mm

Table 4-1. This chart shows the standard minimum width for dressed lumber as compared to the nominal width.

Nominal Thickness (Inches)	Standard Thickness (Inches)	Standard Thickness (Millimeters)
1	$\frac{3}{4}$	19 mm
$1\frac{1}{4}$	1	25 mm
$1\frac{1}{2}$	$1\frac{1}{4}$	32 mm
2	$1\frac{1}{2}$	38 mm

Table 4-2. This chart shows the standard minimum thickness for dressed lumber as compared to its nominal thickness.

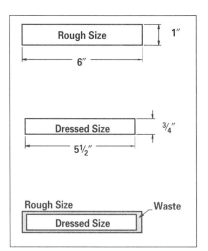

Illus. 4-2. The sizes of nominal (rough) versus surfaced (dressed) lumber.

SURFACED 4 SIDES LUMBER

Nominal Size (Inches)	Standard Size (Inches)	Standard Size (Metric)
1 x 1	$\frac{3}{4}$ x $\frac{3}{4}$	19 x 19
1 x 2	$\frac{3}{4}$ x $1\frac{1}{2}$	19 x 38
1 x 3	$\frac{3}{4}$ x $2\frac{1}{2}$	19 x 63
1 x 4	$\frac{3}{4}$ x $3\frac{1}{2}$	19 x 89
1 x 6	$\frac{3}{4}$ x $5\frac{1}{2}$	19 x 140
1 x 8	$\frac{3}{4}$ x $7\frac{1}{4}$	19 x 184
1 x 10	$\frac{3}{4}$ x $9\frac{1}{4}$	19 x 235
1 x 12	$\frac{3}{4}$ x $11\frac{1}{4}$	19 x 286
2 x 2	$1\frac{1}{2}$ x $1\frac{1}{2}$	38 x 38
2 x 4	$1\frac{1}{2}$ x $3\frac{1}{2}$	38 x 89
2 x 6	$1\frac{1}{2}$ x $5\frac{1}{2}$	38 x 140
2 x 8	$1\frac{1}{2}$ x $7\frac{1}{4}$	38 x 184
2 x 10	$1\frac{1}{2}$ x $9\frac{1}{4}$	38 x 235
2 x 12	$1\frac{1}{2}$ x $11\frac{1}{4}$	38 x 286

Table 4-3. This chart shows the minimal actual sizes of lumber that has been dressed on four sides as compared to its nominal sizes.

you will always be charged for the nominal dimension of the board they started with, not the final size. In most cases, dressed lumber will be available at your local home improvement store, while rough lumber can be found at specialty lumber outlets.

The price of lumber is normally based on its nominal dimensions.

Lumber is sold either by the linear foot or by the board foot (bf), which is 144 cubic inches (1 inch thick x 12 inches wide x 12 inches thick). If the wood you buy is sold by the linear foot, its price will vary, depending on its width and thickness. Nevertheless, its price will usually be based on its cost per board foot. A 1 x 6-inch x 8-foot nominal board has 4

bf (Illus. 4-4). This is calculated by multiplying the nominal thickness by the nominal width by the length in inches, and dividing this number by 144. If you multiply by the length in feet, divide by 12 instead. For example,

$$\frac{1 \times 6 \times 96''}{144} = 4bf$$

or

$$\frac{1 \times 6 \times 8'}{12} = 4bf$$

It is common for boards over a certain width and thickness to be priced at a premium. If you are buying lumber that will be dressed by the supplier for you, it's a good idea to ask if the price is for rough or dressed stock, because some may quote their prices for rough stock and others may quote their prices for dressed boards.

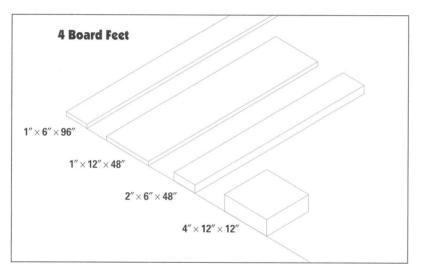

Illus. 4-4. Comparing the sizes of boards which all contain four board feet of lumber.

Illus. 4-5. Various types of wood products that are used on some of the projects in this book. From left to right, they are: 3/4-inch-thick birch plywood; 3/4-inch-thick veneer-core utility plywood; 3/4-inch-thick glued-up panel; 3/4-inch-thick veneered particleboard; 1/4-inch-thick veneered particleboard; and 1/4-inch-thick Masonite.

OTHER WOOD PRODUCTS

Plywood

There are various other wood products that can be used for some of the projects in this book (Illus. 4-5). Plywood is a versatile product that is available in panels that range in size from 18 x 36 inches to 48 x 96 inches (i.e., 4 x 8 feet), and in thickness from 1/8 to 3/4 inch (Illus. 4-6). It is available in utility and finished grades. Finished grades have a high-quality veneer on at least one side to match most solid-lumber species.

Plywood panels are often used where wide pieces of wood are required. They are a less expensive alternative to using solid, glued-up wood panels. However, they are less durable because their face veneers can be easily damaged and aren't easy to repair. Also, the edges of the panels have to be covered with either molding or veneer or hidden by the design of your project.

The primary advantage of plywood panels from a design point of view is that they are dimensionally stable. A large panel of plywood or other sheet stock won't expand and contract with the change in humidity as much as solid lumber will. This feature, as well as the lower cost of plywood panels, is why they are frequently used for large wood surfaces. The thinner $\frac{1}{8}$- and $\frac{1}{4}$-inch panels are perfect for the backs of projects like bookcases and night tables, as well as the bottom of smaller drawers.

When cutting plywood panels, be careful to avoid splintering, which occurs much more easily than with solid wood. Use fine-tooth blades where possible. Keep the good side of the panel down when using a jigsaw, and the good side up when using a handsaw.

Masonite

This hard, man-made panel (Illus. 4-6) is cheap and useful for the bottoms of small drawers and the backs of projects where it will be painted or won't show. It is usually available in $\frac{1}{8}$- and $\frac{1}{4}$-inch thicknesses only.

Particleboard

Particleboard is made from chipped wood that is glued together under pressure to form a panel. Like plywood, particleboard is available in many sizes and thicknesses. Particleboard can be bought without any surface covering, laminated with melamine on both sides (commonly

used for shelving), or with a quality wood veneer on one side and a lesser-quality veneer on the other. This latter version is called a particleboard core veneer panel (Illus. 4-7). It is not as durable as plywood, but is usually less expensive.

Because of how it is made, particleboard is more difficult to join than solid wood or even plywood. When screwing into its edge, it is important to use long screws and drill pilot

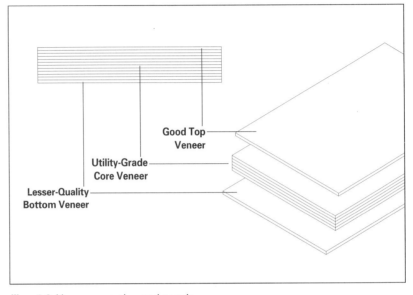

Illus. 4-6. Veneer-core plywood panels.

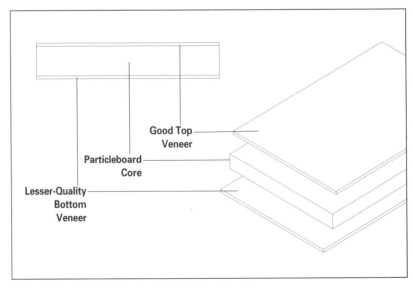

Illus. 4-7. Particleboard core panels.

holes to prevent the panel from bulging out. Because it isn't as strong as solid wood, you should avoid using it for anything other than large pieces that won't receive a lot of stress at the joints.

Glued-Up panels

These solid-wood panels are available in widths from 8 to 24 inches and lengths from 2 to 8 feet. Various manufacturers provide them in different woods, with pine being the most common. They are manufactured from narrow boards glued together to the required width and crosscut to length, giving you an accurate, square panel to start from. They are ideal for projects where you prefer solid wood to plywood, either for durability or to avoid the problem of exposed edges with plywood or particleboard. They are more expensive than plywood, because they are made from solid wood. Work with them just as you would with any other board.

Moldings

Moldings come in a wide variety of shapes and styles for many different decorative uses. They are usually only available in certain species of wood, so keep this in mind when selecting wood for a project where you want the molding to match. Molding pieces can be combined to give different effects: to hide the edges of both solid wood and plywood, to create false raised panels, or to add a routed effect to the edge of boards without using a router.

If you plan on painting your project, finger-jointed molding is ideal, as it is less costly than clear molding. Finger-jointed moldings are made at the factory by joining various scrap lengths of wood together with a tight finger joint before milling the molding.

SELECTING MATERIALS FOR OUTDOOR PROJECTS

Which type of wood material—as well as fasteners, glue, and finish—you decide to use will be influenced by whether the project will be used indoors or outdoors. Indoor projects aren't exposed to the weather, so special attention is rarely needed except when the project will receive excessive wear. In that case, a harder wood and more durable finish will be required.

For outdoor projects, the selection of materials is critical. A finish formulated for outdoor projects is a necessity, and even then, the wood you choose should also be able to stand up to the weather.

Cedar is the best overall choice for outdoor use, because it has a natural ability to resist rot and fungus. Also, if left natural, cedar weathers well and turns a soft gray color over time. Pine is another good choice, but doesn't resist rot, and should be kept off the ground. Pine should be covered with an outdoor finish, which may be a clear stain or paint, depending on your preference and the use of the project. Check with your local supplier for suitable finishes. There are other species of wood suitable for outdoor construction that may be available in your area. Check with your local supplier for the best choice.

Whether you use nails or screws on your project, it is important that they are specially made for outdoor use. Outdoor nails are usually galvanized, while screws may be brass, stainless steel, or coated. Don't be tempted to use standard steel screws or nails; you will end up with rusted fasteners and rust stains on your project.

For outdoor projects requiring glue, use a waterproof formulation. Standard white or yellow glues sold for woodworking will dissolve in water even after they have dried. Waterproof glues will withstand water and moisture. Not only will they maintain their bond, but they will not run and ooze out of joints. Check with your local supplier for suitable glues.

BUYING WOOD AND GETTING IT CUT

Sources of Wood

Most major home improvement outlets carry predressed dimensioned lumber, plywood products, glued panels, and other wood products. The selections may vary depending on the outlet's local demand, so be sure to ask in advance if you are looking for something they don't regularly carry.

Lumberyards that cater to retail buyers often have predressed lumber in their warehouses. If they don't, you may have to place your order in advance so they can dress the rough lumber. Be aware that the prices quoted may be for rough undressed lumber, with an additional charge to have it dressed to standard dimensions.

Some outlets will sell common sizes by the linear foot. This is often simply a matter of convenience. However, be sure to verify this when you are looking for prices.

Lumberyards will often dress or cut your lumber to your own specifications if you need a certain size for a specific project. Because the process of dressing, jointing, and planing lumber isn't exact, you should always check the boards before using them, just in case there are slight variations in size that you need to take into account while you are constructing your project.

If you don't have a retail source of lumber nearby, you may be able to find a professional cabinetmaker or woodworker who is willing to sell wood. In this case, he would be well set up to dress it to your needs. Mail-order lumber is available, with the caveat that you don't know exactly what you are getting until you receive it. Due to its weight, the cost of shipping will certainly make it more expensive. However, in some areas, this may be the only reasonable way to get some types of wood. When ordering, be very careful to make sure the company you deal with fully understands your needs. Be as specific as you can about what you expect to receive when talking to the mail-order company.

SERVICES YOU MAY NEED

There are a few basic services that you may need even if you are able to buy standard sizes of dressed lumber in your area. Ripping, jointing, and power-planing are examples of such services. While you can do all of these jobs with a handsaw and plane, you may sometimes find it easier to pay a little to have it done for you.

Lumberyards and home improvement stores often provide cutting services at a nominal charge when you buy your wood. This service is often very handy, especially with large items such as plywood. Carrying a 4 x 8 sheet of plywood home may be impossible for you, but, for a small price, a few cuts may make it possible. This service is often charged by the cut, with different costs for different types of materials or the nature of the cut.

5
SANDING AND FINISHING TECHNIQUES

SANDING

Sanding is an important part of every project. Even smooth wood should be sanded before finishing, to ensure that you actually have a smooth, clean surface for your finish. Wood that has been planed by machine may feel smooth, but a close look will reveal the small ridges left behind from the cutters.

Hand-sanding can be done in two ways (Illus. 5-1). One is simply with a folded piece of sandpaper. The oth-er is with the sandpaper wrapped around a block of wood or commercially available sanding block.

When sanding a flat surface or the edge of a board, use a sanding block to ensure the sandpaper is held flat against the wood. This is especially important where you want to avoid rounding corners. Folded sandpaper is ideal for sanding curved surfaces or for rounding over edges and corners. Fold a piece small enough to hold comfortably. To sand curved surfaces, such as those made with your jigsaw, you can also wrap the sandpaper around a large dowel.

Sandpaper

Sandpaper is basically paper with a sharp-grit abrasive glued to it. The most common types of grit are silicon carbide, aluminum oxide, and garnet. Three factors influence the performance of these grits: their hardness, toughness, and tendency to fracture.

Silicon carbide is the hardest abrasive, yet it is also quite brittle and fractures readily in use. It constantly presents sharp cutting surfaces to the wood, but wears down very fast, especially with power-sanding. This feature is attractive for fine work or sanding hard finishes, but doesn't make it the best choice as a general-use sandpaper.

Aluminum oxide is almost as hard as silicon carbide, but it is much tougher, slowly wearing down instead of constantly fracturing into fresh cutting edges. Aluminum oxide's durability makes it the best choice for use on power sanders.

Garnet is the softest of the three materials, and is the most widely available sandpaper. It rates in toughness between silicon carbide and aluminum oxide, and it does have the attractive feature of fracturing as it wears, creating fresh cutting edges. For power-sanding, garnet is less durable than aluminum oxide, but more durable than silicon carbide. It is an excellent sandpaper for hand-sanding, and is still commonly used for power-sanding.

Sandpaper is sold in standard sheets or specialty sizes to suit power sanders with grit sizes of 50, 80, 100, 120, 150, 180, 220, and even 360. These grits are loosely grouped into

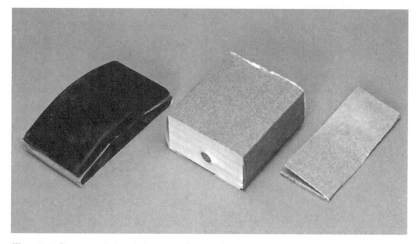
Illus. 5-1. Commercial and shop-made sanding blocks and folded sandpaper.

five categories (Table 5-1). While it may be convenient to buy sandpaper packaged in the categories listed, try to find a supplier who sells individual sheets. This way, you will be sure of having the correct range of grits.

Sanding Techniques

You should start sanding dressed wood with 100-grit sandpaper and end with 220 grit, stepping through the grit sizes in between for the best results. Many sandpapers above 220 grit are sold for specialty applications, and are seldom used on bare wood.

Begin by examining all surfaces. Make a note of areas that may require special attention or a coarser grit, and deal with these before beginning the sanding process. Depending on the project, you may want to do most of the sanding before assembly. Be sure to sand all the components to the same grit.

Whether you use a power sander or do your sanding by hand, maintain an even pressure with constant motion and apply this uniformly across the surface. Avoid putting pressure on the edges of the sanding

pad to deal with a trouble spot. This may take care of the trouble spot, but will make your surface visibly uneven. Instead, sand down a larger area; this will be less noticeable once the finish is applied.

To avoid rounding the edges of your work, stop when the pad is less than halfway over the edge and either lift it off or reverse direction. Don't forget to sand the end grain, particularly if you will be staining or finishing with oil. The end grain will darken more than the face grain if you haven't flattened the fibers by sanding. Use a steady hand to avoid rounding over the edges, and sand in one direction only, to help reduce the porosity of the end grain.

Step through the grits without skipping any, and check the surface with a light each time to make sure you have removed all scratches from the previous grit. Carefully brush or blow off all the dust between grits. This will prevent a stray grit left by the previous sandpaper from becoming lodged between the work and your sandpaper, causing deep scratches. Also brush or blow off the dust before applying your finish.

FINISHING TECHNIQUES

The finish you apply will give your project both protection and character. Which finish you use will largely be a matter of personal preference.

If you plan on using a water-based stain or a finish coat, be careful to eliminate all sources of wax and silicone when building your project. They can cause fish-eye and other problems with the application of water-based finishes, so use a clean cloth to wipe the dust from your project while sanding. Do *not* use a com-

mercially available tack cloth, because it could contain wax.

Before applying any finish, you should decide if you need a wood filler or not. Wood fillers are used to fill in the large pores in woods such as oak and ash before a stain or finish coat is applied. It is a matter of preference. If you want a totally smooth finish, then a wood filler is necessary. If you want the texture of the natural grain and pores to show through, then you don't need a wood filler. If you do use a wood filler, check for compatibility with your stain or finish coat before using it on the project.

Unless you are painting, any glue spots or squeeze-out on the project must be removed before you apply a stain or finish coat, because the glue will inhibit penetration and adherence of the finish and will cause a discoloration.

In almost all cases with finish coats, applying it in a number of thin coats is better than a fewer number of thick coats. Allow each coat to dry properly in accordance with the manufacturer's instructions before applying a subsequent coat. Then sand lightly with a very fine grit. Wipe the surface clean between coats to eliminate bubbles or other blemishes in the finish. Keep an eye out for any drips or runs in the finish.

Different finish manufacturers recommend different application tools (Illus. 5-2), be they bristle brushes, foam paintbrushes, or short-bristled paint pads. If you use bristle brushes, use tapered synthetic brushes that are not flayed at their tips, because flayed tips can trap air and introduce bubbles into your finish. The tapered end of the brush will apply the finish smoother than a flat-tipped brush will. Foam brushes

SANDPAPER GRITS	
Designation	*Grit-Size Range*
Extra coarse	36–40
Coarse	50–60
Medium	80–100
Fine	120–150
Extra fine	180–220

Table 5-1. Sandpaper is commonly sold by designation rather than by grit. This chart shows the typical grit-size range for each category.

are a popular alternative, and work well for most finishes.

A good applicator for applying finishes to flat surfaces is a short-bristled paint pad, which allows you to apply the finish smoothly and efficiently.

If you don't expect to use the entire container of finish for your project, pour only what you need into a separate container, to avoid the possibility of contaminating the unused portion.

The application suggestions here will apply to most situations. However, some products may be formulated differently and should be applied in a very specific way, so you should read and follow the manufacturer's instructions closely. If you deviate from the instructions, test the finish on a scrap piece before working on your project.

Paint

Many woodworkers feel that painting wood hides its beauty. However, if you have a specific look you are trying to achieve or decor you are matching, then painting may be the right thing to do. If you do paint your project, don't spend too much money on expensive, high-grade lumber. Before you paint, make sure that there aren't any flaws in the wood which will show through the paint, such as loose or sappy knots. Paint is available that is specifically formulated for wood and can be found in traditional oil-or water-based formulations.

Stain

Stain is usually applied under a clear finish coat. However, some brands combine the stain with a finish coat, eliminating the second step. When applying stains, it is important that the wood be properly sanded and the stain applied carefully and evenly.

You should always practice on a scrap piece of wood before tackling your project, since it is very difficult to recover from mistakes when using stains. Also, the look of the stain on your particular wood may be different from what is shown on the can or on sample panels in the store. With softwood such as pine or poplar, you should apply a wood conditioner before applying the stain, since these woods are notorious for taking the stain unevenly or leaving blotches.

When selecting a stain, try to find a gel stain. It is easier to use than penetrating stains, because it takes longer to penetrate the wood and gives you a little more time to work with it.

Penetrating stains can be applied with a synthetic brush, foam brush, short-bristled paint pad, or a rag. Apply the stain liberally, allowing it to penetrate for no longer than a couple of minutes. If necessary, you can reapply or blend the stain on the surface if there are parts of the wood which take the stain differently. You may also be able to lighten the surfaces slightly by wiping off the stain with a clean, damp rag without allowing it to penetrate, or, darken the surface by applying more stain to the area and leaving it for a longer period of time. With some products, you may have to wait for the first coat of stain to dry before applying a second coat if you are trying to achieve a darker finish. Before the stain dries, wipe off all excess.

Gel stains are easier to apply, because they penetrate the wood more slowly. Apply them with a cloth in liberal coats with the grain. Wipe off the excess immediately with the grain, to achieve the desired effect. To darken the finish, either allow the stain to penetrate longer or reapply it. As with penetrating stains, you can work on specific areas to better blend areas that appear to be taking the stain differently.

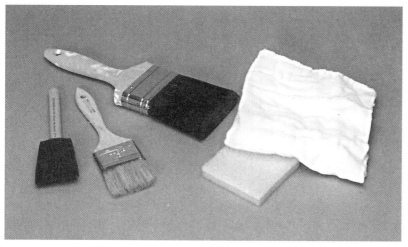

Illus. 5-2. Applicators for finishes. Shown here are a foam paintbrush, a natural-bristle disposable brush, a synthetic-fiber brush, a paint pad, and a rag.

Finish Coat

Most finish coats can be applied over a stain or as the only finish. Common finishes include drying oils, varnish, and polyurethane. Each is described below. Other finishes are available; however, they are specialized or require professional application. The finishes each have their own characteristics, benefits, and disadvantages. Assess each project separately to determine which finish is the most appropriate for the project's intended use.

Drying oils Drying oils include the popular Danish oil and polymerized tung oil. They are very-easy-to-apply oil-based finishes that will dry without feeling oily. Drying oils work by penetrating the wood rather than adhering to the surface, and will impart a natural feel to wood. Unfortunately, they are not very resistant to water or excessive wear and will require periodic reapplication to maintain their look. One very significant advantage is that you can easily repair drying oils simply by applying new coats to the damaged area.

The easiest way to apply the oil is with a rag. Apply the oil liberally, allowing it to penetrate for a while before wiping it off. Check the manufacturer's label for the finish's drying time, since some formulations will dry quite quickly. Permit each coat to dry completely before adding another. Apply at least three coats, buffing the surface with a cloth in between coats.

Polyurethane A very durable finish, polyurethane has a bad reputation for giving a plastic look and feel to wood. This is largely a result of applying it too thickly rather than building up several very thin coats. It is widely available in the traditional oil-based formulation or as a water-based finish. Water-based polyurethane finishes are as good as the oil-based versions. They also are better for the environment, have less odor, and easily clean up with water.

When applying polyurethane, be careful with vertical surfaces. In such situations, runs and sags are very easy to get, and are hard to see when you are applying a clear finish. Apply thin coats, sand the surface lightly with fine sandpaper, and wipe it with a cloth between coats. Be sure to apply the finish in a dust-free area with very little draft, but suitable ventilation.

Varnish The easiest formulation to use is a gelled rubbing varnish. This method requires a little extra effort, but will produce a very traditional look. Apply the varnish with a lint-free cloth, rubbing it into the wood in sections. As you rub, the finish will build up, and the friction will increase until the finish is only slightly tacky. Once one coat has been applied, add another one or two in order to properly build up a protective finish.

6
PROJECTS

USING THE PROJECT PLANS

All the projects in this book have detailed drawings and step-by-step instructions. Some information for specific techniques, such as drilling pilot holes, are not repeated in the instructions but are covered in preceding chapters.

The drawings and the step-by-step instructions are meant to be used together. When building the project, always refer to the drawing at each step, as it may provide you with additional information. It is best to read the instructions all the way through before beginning each project.

The cutting lists identify the finished sizes required. While the projects are designed to use standard dimensions, your wood may deviate slightly from the standard. Always verify the dimensions of the wood you use before beginning a project, and adjust any dimensions as required.

Sanding and finishing instructions are not given in the step-by-step instructions, as this would be very repetitive. Chapter 5 will provide you with enough information for any project.

Take a look at the chart included on this page. It lists the tools needed for each of the projects and their difficulty rating.

DIFFICULTY OF PROJECTS, AND TOOLS NEEDED

Project	Page	Handsaw	Hammer	Screwdriver	Drill	Jigsaw	Hand Plane	Miter Box	Difficulty
Activity Center	141	x		x	x			o*	3
Airplane	86	x		x	x	x			1
Baseball Equipment Organizer	89		x	x					3
Bird Feeder	69	x	x		x		o		2
Birdhouse	79	x	x	x	x				2
CD Holder	95	x		x	x			o	2
Children's Chair	117	x		x	x			o	3
Children's Table	113	x		x	x				3
Clock	92	x			x		o	x	3
Coatrack	132	x			x				1
Cutting Board	122	x				x			1
Display Cabinet	84	x		x	x	x		x	5
Entranceway Bench	99	x		x	x	x			4
Firewood Box	110	x	x	x	x				5
Fold-Up Chair	66	x		x	x			o	3
Footstool	72	x		x	x		x		3
Garden Bench	125	x			x				3
Garden Planter	127	x	x						1
Garden Tray	120	x	x		x			o	2
Kitchen Keeper	136	x		x	x				2
Mailbox	97	x	x	x	x	x	x		2
Night Table	74	x		x	x	x			3
Patio Bench	147	x			x				3
Patio Table	149	x		x	x				3
Recipe Book Holder	134	x		x			o	o	2
Seesaw	129	x		x	x	x			3
Snack Table	144	x		x	x	x			3
Spice Rack	82	x	x	x	x			o	1
Spoon Rack	154	x	x		x	o			2
Step Stool	152	x		x	x				3
Toolbox	105	x		x	x	x			3
Tool Chest	102	x		x	x				5
Under-the Bed Drawer	156	x		x	x				2
Wall Shelf	77	x		x	x	x			2
Window Planter	108	x	x						2
Workbench	138	x	x	x	x				4

* o Means optional.   ** A grade of 5 is most difficult, and 1 is least difficult

FOLD-UP CHAIR

Bring your own chair with you when going to outdoor events. This fold-up chair (Illus. 6-1 and 6-3) is easy to carry and comfortable to sit on.

Tools and Materials Needed

• Handsaw
• Screwdriver
• Drill
• Screws
• Sanding block or drum sander
• Glue

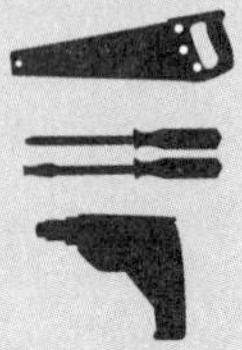

INSTRUCTIONS

1. Cut out the parts with a handsaw (Illus. 6-2).

2. Lightly round over all the corners and edges with a piece of #180 sandpaper folded and held in your hand.

3. Round one end of each chair support with a sanding block or drum sander mounted in your drill. Another option is to use a jigsaw.

Illus. 6-2. Cutting a crosspiece to length with a miter box.

Illus. 6-1. Folding chair.

Cutting List

Part	Qty.	Dimensions	Material
Chair Support	4	¾ x 1½ x 26 inches	Maple
Crosspiece	2	¾ x 1½ x 14 inches	Maple
Crosspiece	11	¾ x 1½ x 14 inches	Pine

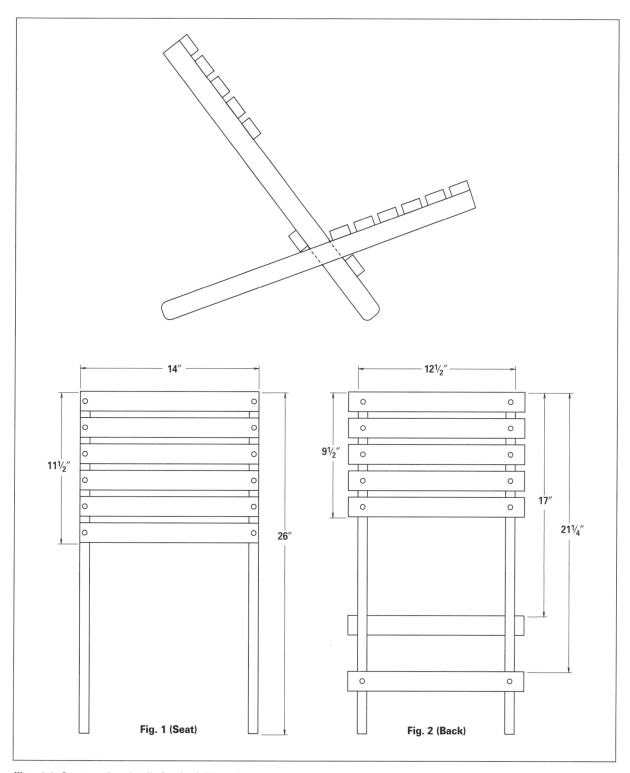

Illus. 6-3. Construction details for the folding chair.

Illus. 6-4. Drilling a countersunk pilot hole at the end of a crosspiece.

4. Drill countersunk pilot holes centered and $\frac{3}{8}$ inch in from the ends on six of the pine crosspieces (Illus. 6-4). You can counterbore the pilot holes and plug them if you prefer. These crosspieces will be used as seat slats.

5. Position the seat slats on two chair supports so their ends are flush and the spacing is even (Fig. 1 in Illus. 6-3). Then drill $\frac{1}{8}$-inch pilot holes $\frac{1}{2}$ inch deep into the chair supports through the pilot holes you previously drilled.

6. Apply glue to the mating surfaces and screw the seat slats onto the supports with $1\frac{1}{4}$-inch-long screws. Check to make sure the assembly is square and allow it to dry.

7. For the seat back (Fig. 2 in Illus. 6-3), drill the pilot holes in the five remaining pine crosspieces $1\frac{1}{8}$ inches in from their ends, as you did for the seat slats.

8. Glue and screw the crosspieces in place for the back. To do this, first lay the seat down with its slats facing up, and then place the next two chair supports between the seat's supports. Lay the cross slats for the back on top (Fig. 2 in Illus. 6-3), and drill $\frac{1}{8}$-inch pilot holes $\frac{1}{2}$ inch deep into the supports. Then apply glue and screw the crosspieces in place with $1\frac{1}{4}$-inch screws. Do the same thing for the two maple crosspieces, making sure they are the same distance from the top on both sides.

Tip

• To prevent the seat and back from binding together when you open them up, place a business card between the chair supports on each side at both ends and in the middle while assembling the chair to make sure there is clearance between the seat and back supports.

References

• Pilot Holes in Chapter 2
• Gluing Up Boards in Chapter 3
• Sanding and Finishing in Chapter 5
• Using Your Plane in Chapter 2

BIRD FEEDER

If you want to attract beautiful birds to your yard, or just help feed the birds in your area, this easy-to-make bird feeder (Illus. 6-5 and 6-7) will fit the bill. It can be mounted on a pole, on a tree, or even to the side of a shed or your house.

Tools and Materials Needed

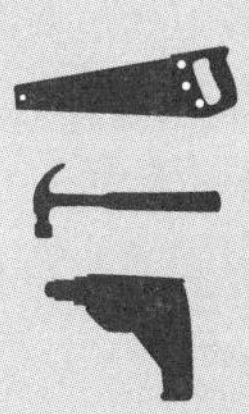

- Handsaw
- Hammer
- Drill
- Waterproof glue
- Sandpaper or drum sander
- Nails
- Glue

Illus. 6-5. Bird feeder.

INSTRUCTIONS

1. Cut out all parts except the side pieces.

2. Cut out the side pieces. To do this, select a 7½-inch-long x 5½-inch-wide board and measure it as indicated in Fig. 3 of Illus. 6-7. Use a straightedge to draw a straight line between the marks, and cut off the waste by cutting to the outside of the line (Illus. 6-6). Repeat this for the second side piece.

Cutting List

Part	Qty.	Dimensions	Material
Top	1	¾ x 7¼ x 13 inches	Cedar
Side	2	¾ x 7¼ x 7½ inches	Cedar
Back	1	¾ x 7¼ x 8 inches	Cedar
Bottom	1	¾ x 5½ x 9½ inches	Cedar
Front ledge	1	¾ x 1½ x 9 ½ inches	Cedar
Side ledge	2	¾ x 1½ x 8 ½ inches	Cedar
Dowel	1	⅜ x 13 inches	Maple
Front	1	⅛ x 6 x 9½ inches	Plexiglas

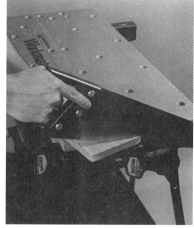

Illus. 6-6. Cutting out a side panel.

69

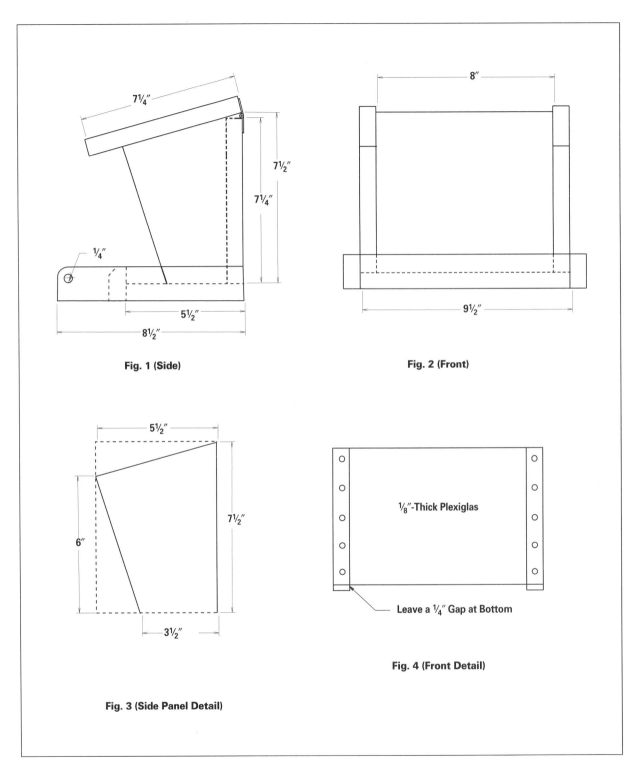

Fig. 1 (Side)

Fig. 2 (Front)

Fig. 3 (Side Panel Detail)

Fig. 4 (Front Detail)

⅛"-Thick Plexiglas

Leave a ¼" Gap at Bottom

Illus. 6-7. Construction details for the bird feeder.

3. Holding the two ledges together, drill a $\frac{1}{4}$-inch hole in the end for the perch and round the corner as shown in Fig. 1 of Illus. 6-4. Use # 100 sandpaper folded up in your hand or with a drum sander mounted in your drill.

4. Nail one side piece onto the end of the back piece so that the back is flush at the bottom and the back edge of the side piece. Do the same for the second side.

5. Drill pilot holes and screw the Plexiglas to the front edge of the side pieces (Fig. 4 in Illus. 6-7), leaving a $\frac{1}{4}$-inch space at the bottom to allow the seeds to flow from the reservoir into the feeder tray.

6. Nail the bottom piece to the assembly you just finished so that it is flush at the sides and back.

7. Use a sanding block to create a chamfer on the front ledge, and then nail it to the bottom piece so it is flush on the bottom and both ends.

8. Nail a side ledge onto each side of the bird feeder so that they are flush on the bottom and at the back.

9. Glue the $\frac{3}{8}$-inch dowel into the holes in the side ledges with a waterproof glue.

10. Screw the hinge to the back of the lid and then to the back of the bird feeder.

Tips

• Instead of using a sanding block, you can make the chamfer with a hand plane.
• Apply a "deck" finish to the outside of the bird feeder, but leave the inside bare.

References

• Selecting Materials for Outdoor Projects in Chapter 4

FOOTSTOOL

Combine comfort and storage by building this footstool (Illus. 6-8 and 6-9). It has a sloped, padded top for added comfort, and enough space inside for your favorite books and magazines.

Tools and Materials Needed

- Handsaw
- Screwdriver
- Drill
- Nails or screws
- Hinges
- Glue

INSTRUCTIONS

1. To get the full height of the stool, glue up the sides and back from $5\frac{1}{2}$- and $2\frac{1}{2}$-inch-wide pieces. Cut the pieces at least an inch longer than necessary before gluing them together. Then make sure one end and the outer surface are perfectly flush while gluing them together. When it is dry, cut the piece to length.

2. Cut the legs, and then glue them to the main pieces so that they are flush on the face side and flush with the edge. Clamp them and wait until they dry.

3. Sand the glued-up pieces smooth.

4. On both side pieces, measure $2\frac{1}{2}$ inches down from the top on one edge and join this point with the opposite top corner. Cut off the waste and plane or sand the cut edge smooth. If your boards have a good side, make sure you cut the board so the good side will be facing out once the pieces are assembled.

5. Drill counterbored pilot holes in the ends of the side pieces $\frac{3}{8}$ inch from the edge.

Illus. 6-8. Footstool.

Cutting List

Part	Qty.	Dimensions	Material
Side	2	$\frac{3}{4}$ x 8 x $15\frac{1}{2}$ inches	Oak
Front	1	$\frac{3}{4}$ x 8 x 14 inches	Oak
Back	1	$\frac{3}{4}$ x $5\frac{1}{2}$ x 14 inches	Oak
Bottom	1	$\frac{1}{2}$ x 14 x 14 inches	Oak
Support	4	$\frac{3}{4}$ x $1\frac{1}{2}$ x $9\frac{1}{2}$ inches	Oak
Leg	2	$\frac{3}{4}$ x $2\frac{1}{2}$ x 3 inches	Oak
Leg	2	$\frac{3}{4}$ x $2\frac{1}{2}$ x $2\frac{1}{4}$ inches	Oak
Top	1	$\frac{3}{4}$ x $14\frac{1}{2}$ x $14\frac{1}{2}$ inches	Oak

6. Nail or screw the shelf supports on the inside of each end and side piece so that they are centered end to end and flush with the bottom edge.

7. Assemble the side and end pieces, apply glue to the mating surfaces, carefully drill a pilot hole through each existing counterbored pilot hole, and then screw the pieces together as you go.

8. Sand the edges flush at each corner with a sanding block, and glue screw-hole plugs in place.

9. Apply glue to the top of the shelf supports and put the shelf in place.

10. Use a plane to make an angle on the top of the back piece to match the sides, as shown in Fig. 4 of Illus. 6-9.

11. Cut out a piece of 2-inch foam to match the top. Cover the foam with fabric and tack it in place underneath at least 2 inches in from the edges.

12. Put the top in place and mark the position of the two hinges. Screw them to the underside of the top and then to the top edge of the back piece of the footstool.

Tips

• You can use dowels instead of screws.
• You can use 8½-inch-wide lumber instead of gluing up the 5½- and 2½-inch pieces. The extra ½ inch won't make a difference.
• You can use a jigsaw to add an interesting shape to the legs.

References

• Using a Plane in Chapter 2
• Gluing Up Boards in Chapter 3
• Screw-Hole Plugs in Chapter 2
• Pilot Holes in Chapter 2
• Sanding and Finishing in Chapter 5

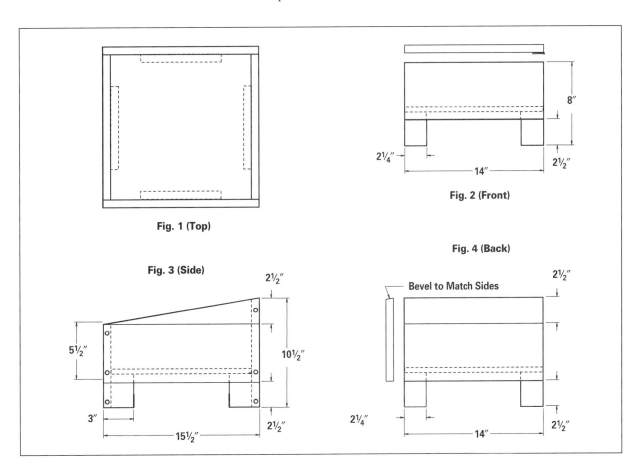

Illus. 6-9. Construction details for the footstool.

NIGHT TABLE

Place this night table (Illus. 6-10 and 6-11) next to your bed, and your favorite reading material will be close at hand. It will also give you a place for your reading light and alarm clock.

Illus. 6-10. Night table.

Tools and Materials Needed

- Handsaw
- Screwdriver
- Drill
- Jigsaw
- Nails
- Sanding block or block plane
- Brads
- Glue

Cutting List

Part	Qty.	Dimensions	Material
Side piece	4	$3/4$ x $5^1/_2$ x $23^1/_4$ inches	Pine
Top piece	2	$3/4$ x $5^1/_2$ x 17 inches	Pine
Back	1	$1/8$ x $16^1/_4$ x $20^1/_4$ inches	Plywood
Bottom	1	$3/4$ x $15^1/_2$ x 11 inches	Plywood
Face piece	2	$3/4$ x $1^1/_2$ x 17 inches	Pine
Drawer front	1	$3/4$ x $5^1/_2$ x 17 inches	Pine
Drawer end	2	$3/4$ x $3^1/_2$ x $13^7/_8$ inches	Pine
Drawer side	2	$3/4$ x $3^1/_2$ x $10^1/_2$ inches	Pine
Drawer bottom	1	$1/4$ x $10^1/_2$ x $15^3/_8$ inches	Pine
Front support	2	$3/4$ x $1^1/_2$ x 14 inches	Pine
Side support	4	$3/4$ x $1^1/_2$ x $10^3/_4$ inches	Pine

INSTRUCTIONS

1. Make the top and side panels by gluing up $5^1/_2$-inch boards at least 1 inch longer than needed (Illus. 6-11). Make sure one end is perfectly flush and even; then cut the second end to size once the boards are dry.

2. Cut the side pieces. Then, using a compass, draw the $1/2$ circle at the bottom of the side pieces and cut the circles out with a jigsaw. Sand the cut edge smooth by hand using #180 sandpaper folded up or with a drum sander mounted in your drill.

3. Join the top and sides with dowels. For the top, drill four evenly spaced dowel holes on the underside at each end. The holes should be $3/8$ inch in from the end and 1, 6, 11, and 16 inches in from the edge. Drill matched dowel holes in the top edge of both sides, making sure that the best side of the boards will be facing outward.

4. Make the drawer and shelf supports by first drilling counter-

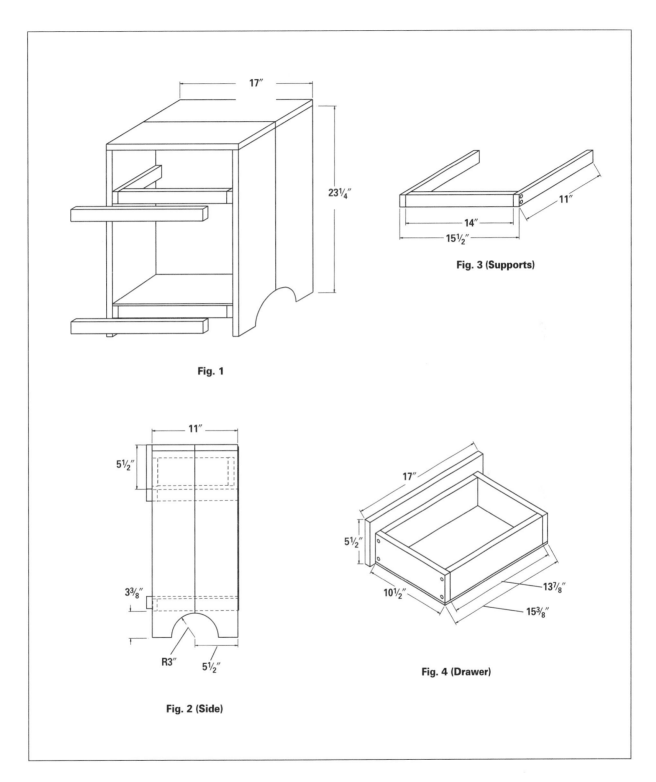

Fig. 1

Fig. 3 (Supports)

Fig. 2 (Side)

Fig. 4 (Drawer)

Illus. 6-11. Construction details for the night table.

sunk pilot holes into one end of each side support, and then screwing the side supports to the front supports so that they are flush on the top and front.

5. Tack the shelf in place on one of the support assemblies with brads so that it is flush at the front and sides. If necessary, trim the shelf to size with a sanding block or block plane after it has been nailed to the support.

6. To install the supports, first drill countersunk pilot holes in the support side pieces, and then screw the two supports in place onto the side pieces 3 $\frac{3}{8}$ inches from the bottom and 5$\frac{1}{2}$ inches from the top, making sure they are flush at the front.

7. Add the top by applying glue to the mating edges of the top and side panels and to the dowel holes. Insert the dowels into the holes in the side panels and place the top over the dowels, pressing them into the matching holes. Make sure the night table is square. Then clamp the top down or set it upright and place books or other items on the top to weight it down while it dries.

8. Screw the face pieces to each support from behind through countersunk pilot holes.

9. Assemble the drawers by screwing the side pieces to the front and back pieces through countersunk pilot holes drilled $\frac{3}{8}$ inch from the edges. Glue and tack the bottom on from underneath with brads, trimming it with a sanding block or block plane if required. Screw the drawer front onto the drawer from inside so that it is centered and flush at the bottom.

10. Add a drawer handle and insert the drawer into the night table.

Tips

• You can buy prelaminated 12-inch-wide panels for the top and sides, adjusting the other measurements as required.
• Instead of using dowels, screw the top onto the sides with counterbored pilot holes and flat screw-hole plugs.
• You don't have to cut the decorative hole in the bottom if you don't own a jigsaw.

References

• Pilot Holes in Chapter 2
• Gluing Up Boards in Chapter 3
• Sanding and Finishing in Chapter 5
• Dowels in Chapter 3

WALL SHELF

This attractive two-tiered shelf (Illus. 6-12 and 6-13) has a bottom hanger for push pins on which keepsakes, reminders, and other special items can be hung, helping to reduce clutter.

Tools and Materials Needed

- Handsaw
- Screwdriver
- Drill
- Jigsaw
- Angle brackets
- #180 sandpaper
- Hooks or thumbtacks
- Glue

Illus. **6-12.** Wall shelf.

INSTRUCTIONS

1. Glue up two 5½-inch-wide boards for each side panel. Cut the 5½-inch pieces at least 1 inch longer than required and glue the boards together with one end and one surface perfectly flush. Once they are dry, cut the panels to length.

2. Trace the shelf and hanger profile on one of the side panels, and then draw the cut-out profile onto the panel.

3. Clamp the two side panels together and cut out the profiles with a jigsaw. If you don't have a blade long enough to cut through both side panels, cut one panel out first and trace it onto the second panel to act as a matching pattern.

4. Sand the edges with a drum sander mounted in your drill. If possible, clamp the side panels together before you sand so that both side panels will be the same when finished.

5. Round over the edges lightly

Cutting List

Part	Qty.	Dimensions	Material
Bottom shelf	1	¾ x 5½ x 24 inches	Pine
Top shelf	1	¾ x 7¼ x 24 inches	Pine
Bottom hanger	1	¾ x 1½ x 24 inches	Pine
Side panel	2	¾ x 8¼ x 17⅜ inches	Pine

with #180 sandpaper folded up and held in your hand.

6. Lay out the holes for the shelves and hanger on the outside surface of each side panel. Drill counterbored pilot holes.

7. Screw the shelves onto the side panels and glue screw-hole plugs into the holes.

8. Use two angle brackets underneath the top shelf to attach it to the wall.

9. Use hooks or thumbtacks to attach things to the bottom hanger.

References

• Gluing Up Boards in Chapter 3
• Pilot Holes in Chapter 2
• Screw-Hole Plugs in Chapter 2
• Sanding and Finishing in Chapter 5

Tips

• You can make this shelf as tall as you want by lengthening the side panels and adding more shelves.
• Position the angle brackets so that you will be mounting your shelf into wall studs. Otherwise, use good wall anchors.
• You can use a 9-inch-wide board instead of gluing up two 6-inch-wide boards.

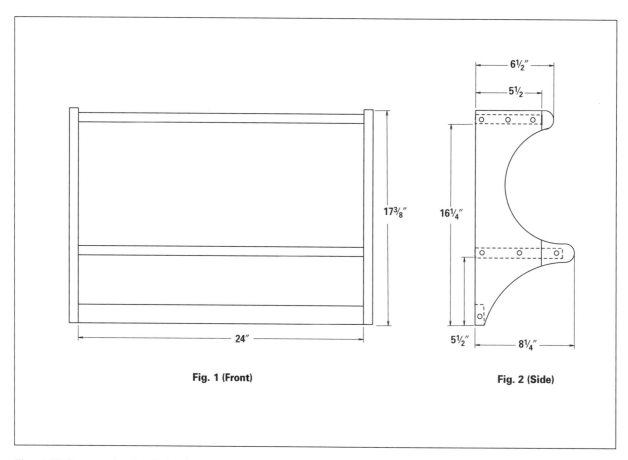

Fig. 1 (Front)

Fig. 2 (Side)

Illus. 6-13. Construction details for the wall shelf.

BIRDHOUSE

This birdhouse (Illus. 6-14 and 6-15) makes an attractive home for small birds. Mount it on a post or a tree at least 8 feet high. Be sure to clean it out once a year after the birds have abandoned it.

Tools and Materials Needed

- Handsaw
- Hammer
- Drill
- Screwdriver
- Screws
- Glue

Illus. 6-14. Birdhouse.

Cutting List

Part	Qty.	Dimensions	Material
Front	1	$3/4 \times 5\frac{1}{2} \times 11\frac{1}{4}$ inches	Cedar
Back	1	$3/4 \times 5\frac{1}{2} \times 12\frac{1}{4}$ inches	Cedar
Side	2	$3/4 \times 5\frac{1}{2} \times 9\frac{1}{2}$ inches	Cedar
Roof piece	2	$3/4 \times 5\frac{1}{2} \times 9\frac{1}{2}$ inches	Cedar
Roof peak	1	$3/4 \times 3/4 \times 10\frac{1}{2}$ inches	Cedar
Roof corner	2	$3/4 \times 1\frac{1}{2} \times 1\frac{1}{2}$ inches	Cedar
Bottom	1	$3/4 \times 5\frac{1}{2} \times 4$ inches	Cedar

INSTRUCTIONS

1. Cut out the parts with a handsaw.

2. Mark the peak on the front and back pieces by marking the center of their tops and $8\frac{1}{2}$ inches up on each side. Draw a line joining the marks between the sides and the top. This should result in a 90-degree angle at the peak, as shown in Fig. 1a in Illus. 6-15.

3. Use a handsaw to cut the corner pieces off, sawing to the waste side of the lines.

4. Make a mark on one edge of each of the two side pieces one inch down from the top and use a straightedge to draw a line from this mark to the top of the opposite side. This is shown in Fig. 2 in Illus. 6-15.

5. Cut the waste off with a handsaw, keeping to the waste side of the lines.

6. Mark the center of the hole in the front piece and drill it out with a $1\frac{1}{8}$-inch hole saw. Use a

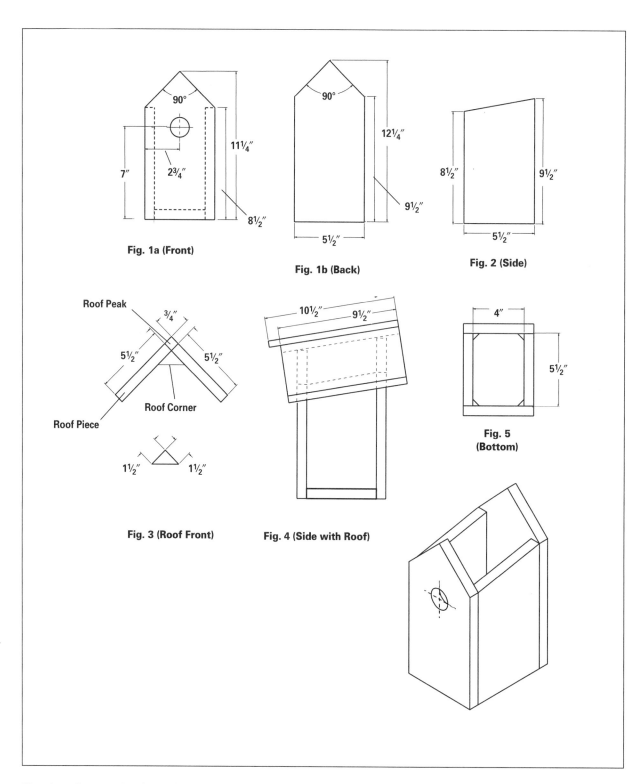

Illus. 6-15. Construction details for the birdhouse.

backing board when you drill, to prevent splintering.

7. Nail the front and back pieces to the side pieces so that their bottoms and edges are flush.

8. Nail the ¾ x ¾-inch roof peak to one of the roof pieces so it is flush at one end. Then nail it to the second roof piece so that the roof is at a 45-degree angle. Next, nail the two roof corners in place so they are flush with the front and back edges.

9. Nail the roof to the top edges of the front and back pieces, as shown in Fig. 4 of Illus. 6-15.

10. Insert the bottom and screw it in place with two screws on each side, but not on the front or back. Use pilot holes to prevent splitting. Using screws will allow you to remove the bottom once a year for cleaning.

Tips

• You can use pine instead of cedar.
• Drill pilot holes for the nails, to reduce the possibility of splitting.

References

• Selecting Materials for Outdoor Projects in Chapter 4

SPICE RACK

Keep your spices handy with this simple spice rack (Illus. 6-16 and 6-17). Leave it on the counter or mount it on the wall in your kitchen.

Tools and Materials Needed

- Handsaw
- Hammer
- Screwdriver
- Drill
- Screws
- Rubber buttons
- #180 sandpaper
- Glue
- Screw-hole plugs

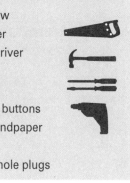

Illus. 6-16. Spice rack.

INSTRUCTIONS

1. Cut out the parts with a handsaw.

2. Drill twelve $\frac{3}{8}$-inch holes $\frac{1}{2}$ inch deep in the side pieces $\frac{1}{2}$ inch in from the edges and $2\frac{3}{4}$ inches apart, starting $1\frac{1}{2}$ inches from the bottom. This is shown in Fig. 2 of Illus. 6-17.

3. Drill two counterbored pilot holes $\frac{3}{8}$ inch from the bottom and $\frac{3}{8}$ inch in from each edge of the side pieces on the opposite side of the holes you just drilled.

4. Sand all edges with #180 sandpaper, and sand a chamfer around the ends of each dowel to ease their entry into the holes.

5. Hold the bottom and one side piece together so they are flush at their bottoms and sides, and then drill a pilot hole into the bottom piece through the pilot hole in the side piece. Screw the pieces together with $1\frac{1}{4}$-inch screws.

Cutting List

Part	Qty.	Dimensions	Material
Side	2	$\frac{3}{4}$ x $2\frac{1}{2}$ x $17\frac{1}{2}$ inches	Oak
Bottom	1	$\frac{3}{4}$ x $2\frac{1}{2}$ x 12 inches	Oak
Dowel	12	$\frac{3}{8}$ x $12\frac{3}{4}$ inches	Hardwood

6. Glue the dowels into all the holes in one side piece and put glue into all the holes of the other side piece.

7. Carefully position the second side piece over the dowels, using a block and hammer to gently force the dowels into the holes. Screw the side piece onto the bottom.

8. Glue screw-hole plugs into the screw holes and add rubber buttons to the bottom.

References

- Pilot Holes in Chapter 2
- Screw-Hole Plugs in Chapter 2
- Dowels in Chapter 3
- Using a Drill in Chapter 2

Tips

- Make the spice rack as tall as needed to hold your spice bottles.
- You can use dowels instead of counterbored pilot holes.
- Test-fit the assembly with the dowels in place before gluing it.
- Use a drill depth stop when drilling the ½-inch-deep hole, to prevent drilling all the way through.

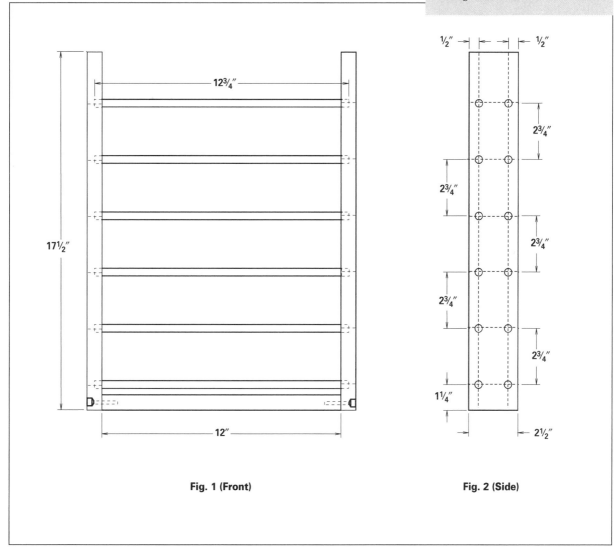

Fig. 1 (Front)   **Fig. 2 (Side)**

Illus. 6-17. Construction details for the spice rack.

DISPLAY CABINET

Whether you have a bare wall to fill or a beautiful collection to display, this display cabinet (Illus. 6-18 and 6-19) will suit your needs. Its adjustable glass shelves allow lots of light into the cabinet, and will suit both small and large items.

Tools and Materials Needed

- Handsaw
- Screwdriver
- Drill
- Jigsaw
- Brads
- Screws
- Shelf pins
- Glue
- Hinges

Illus. 6-18. Display cabinet.

Cutting List

Part	Qty.	Dimensions	Material
Side	2	$3/4 \times 4^1/2 \times 35^3/4$ inches	Maple
Top/Bottom	2	$3/4 \times 5^1/2 \times 23^3/4$ inches	Maple
Back	1	$1/4 \times 23 \times 35$ inches	Plywood
Stile	2	$3/4 \times 1^1/2 \times 35^5/8$ inches	Maple
Rail	2	$3/4 \times 2^1/2 \times 19^3/4$ inches	Maple
Shelf	5	$3/16 \times 4^3/8 \times 21^1/8$ inches	Glass
Front	1	$1/8 \times 19^5/8 \times 30^1/2$ inches	Tempered glass

INSTRUCTIONS

1. Cut out the parts with a handsaw.

2. Lightly mark a line on the inside of each side piece $3/4$ inch in from each edge. Starting $3^1/2$ inches from the top, use your square and make a light mark, crossing both lines every 2 inches. This will keep the shelf pins lined up on both sides (Fig. 3 in Illus. 6-19).

3. Use a drill bit to drill holes $1/2$ inch deep into the side pieces where the lines cross, to accommodate the shelf pins you bought.

4. To assemble the cabinet, first drill two countersunk pilot holes at the ends of the top and bottom pieces $3/8$ inch from the end and 1 inch in from each edge. Next, apply glue to the mating surfaces, carefully line them up so they are flush at their fronts and ends, and drill a $1/8$-inch pilot hole through each existing countersunk pilot hole. Screw the pieces together as you go. Make sure the assembly is square either by checking it with a large framing square or by measuring the diagonals from corner to corner. Adjust the assembly until both diagonals are the same measurement.

5. Nail the back onto the cabinet using brads. There should be a $\frac{1}{4}$-inch gap all around.

6. Assemble the cabinet-door frame pieces onto the cabinet to ensure all the pieces are the correct sizes. Adjust the lengths of the pieces if necessary so that the door is flush with the sides and there is a $\frac{1}{16}$-inch gap at the top and bottom.

7. Drill matching dowel holes into the ends of the rails and on the inside edge of the stiles. Use a dowel jig or centers to get matching holes.

8. Apply glue to the mating surfaces and dowel holes, insert the dowels, and clamp them to dry. Check that the assembly is square before leaving it to dry.

9. Miter-cut the $\frac{1}{2}$-inch cove molding to fit inside the door frame (Fig. 2 in Illus. 6-19). Then glue and tack it in place with brads. Install the glass and screw on the glass stops from inside the frame.

10. Install hinges on the cabinet door and mount it to the cabinet. Install a catch and add a knob to the door.

11. Add the shelf pins and glass shelves.

Tips

• Use dowels instead of screws for the cabinet.
• You can use a lap joint for the door frame instead of a doweled butt joint.
• Use a drill depth stop when drilling the $\frac{1}{2}$-inch-deep holes, to prevent drilling all the way through.

References

• Pilot Holes in Chapter 2
• Using a Drill in Chapter 2
• Dowels in Chapter 3

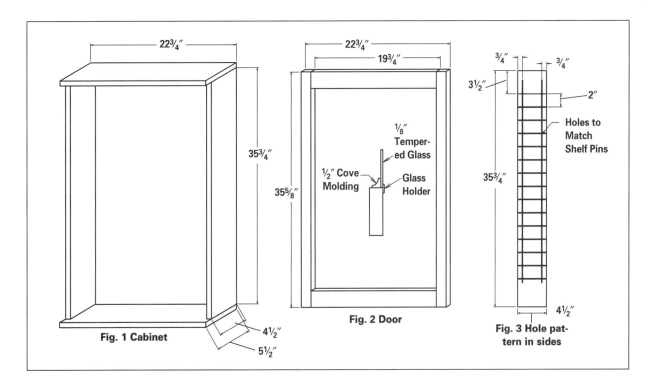

Fig. 1 Cabinet

Fig. 2 Door

Fig. 3 Hole pattern in sides

Illus. 6-19. Construction details for the display cabinet.

AIRPLANE

This airplane (Illus. 6-20 and 6-21) will fascinate your children. You can make it yourself or let your children help you. With rolling wheels and a spinning propeller, it will provide hours of fun.

Tools and Materials Needed

- Handsaw
- Screwdriver
- Drill
- Jigsaw
- Sanding block
- Screws
- Glue
- #180 Sandpaper

Illus. 6-20. Airplane.

Cutting List

Part	Qty.	Dimensions	Material
Main wing	1	$\frac{1}{2}$ x $3\frac{1}{2}$ x 12 inches	Pine
Tail wing	1	$\frac{1}{2}$ x 2 x 5 inches	Pine
Fuselage	1	$1\frac{1}{2}$ x 5 x 14 inches	Pine
Wheel	2	2 inches in diameter with $\frac{3}{8}$-inch hole	Hardwood
Wheel axle	2	to suit wheels	Hardwood
Propeller	1	$\frac{1}{2}$ x 1 x 3 inches	Pine
Propeller axle	1	same as wheel axles	Hardwood

INSTRUCTIONS

1. Cut out the parts with a handsaw.

2. For the fuselage (Fig. 1 in Illus. 6-21), laminate two $\frac{3}{4}$ x $4\frac{1}{2}$ x 14-inch pieces. Then clamp them together and leave them to dry.

3. Draw the profile of the fuselage on the glued-up piece and cut it out with a jigsaw. Sand the cut edges smooth with a drum sander.

4. Drill the hole for the wheel axles in the sides of the fuselage. Drill the hole for the propeller in the end of the fuselage. Use a drill bit to match the axle diameter.

5. Cut out the main wing (Fig. 2 in Illus. 6-21) from $\frac{1}{2}$-inch-thick pine.

6. Use a large jar lid to mark the line used to round the leading edges, and a small glass to mark the line used to round the trailing edges of the wing.

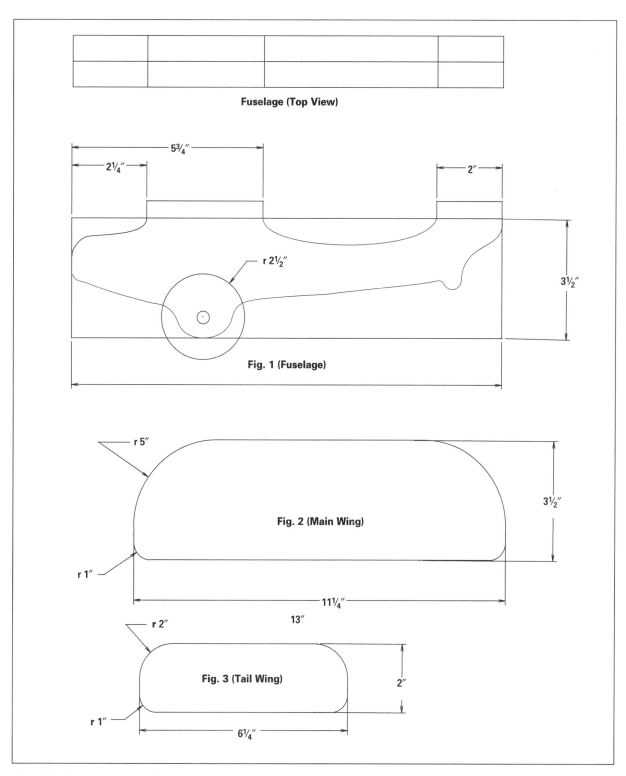

Fuselage (Top View)

Fig. 1 (Fuselage)

Fig. 2 (Main Wing)

Fig. 3 (Tail Wing)

Illus. 6-21. Construction details for the toy airplane.

7. Cut the waste off with a jigsaw, cutting to the outside of the lines.

8. Sand the cut edges with a sanding block and round over all the edges slightly.

9. Repeat the process for the tail wing (Fig. 3 in Illus. 6-21).

10. Drill countersunk pilot holes on the wings. Position them on the fuselage and screw them on.

11. Drill a $\frac{3}{8}$-inch hole in the center of the propeller.

12. Paint the airplane, propeller, and wheels.

13. Put the axle pin through the wheels and glue them into the fuselage. Do the same with the propeller. Before the glue dries, check to make sure that the wheels and propeller turn freely.

References

- Using a Drill in Chapter 2
- Pilot Holes in Chapter 2
- Sanding and Finishing in Chapter 5

Tips

- You can use your own design for the wings and fuselage.
- You can use a $1\frac{1}{2}$-inch-thick piece of pine instead of gluing up the fuselage from $\frac{3}{4}$-inch-thick pieces.
- If you can't find $\frac{1}{2}$-inch pine, you can use standard $\frac{3}{4}$-inch pine instead.

BASEBALL EQUIPMENT ORGANIZER

Keep clutter to a minimum with this baseball equipment organizer (Illus. 6-22 and 6-23), and make sure your favorite bat and glove are within easy reach whenever you need them. If you have more equipment, the organizer can be easily expanded to accommodate everything you have.

Tools and Materials Needed

- Handsaw
- Screwdriver
- Drill
- Hole saw
- Drum sander
- Screws
- Glue

Illus. 6-22. Baseball equipment organizer.

Cutting List

Part	Qty.	Dimensions	Material
Shelf	1	¾ x 5½ x 22¼ inches	Maple
Back	1	¾ x 5½ x 22¼ inches	Maple
Corner brace	1	¾ x 3½ x 3½ inches	Maple

INSTRUCTIONS

1. Cut out all the pieces with a handsaw except the corner brace.

2. Make the corner brace by cutting the piece to size first, and then cutting off one corner, leaving a ½-inch shoulder on both ends.

3. Mark the center of the holes that hold the baseballs on the shelf piece, and drill them out with a 2¼-inch hole saw, using a backing board to prevent splintering.

4. Mark the location of the two holes needed for the bat-holder slot and drill them out with a 1⅛-inch hole saw. Use a backing board for these holes as well.

5. Using a square, draw two lines at each hole between the front edge and each side of the hole. Remove the waste by cutting along these lines to the hole with a handsaw, keeping to the inside of the lines, as shown in Fig. 1 of Illus. 6-23. Sand the cut edges with a drum sander.

6. Drill the countersunk pilot

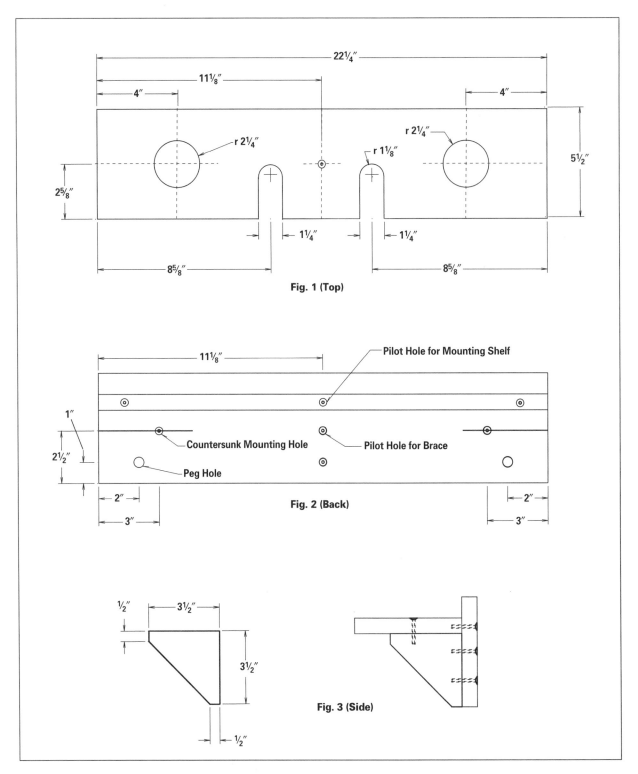

Illus. 6-23. Construction details for the baseball equipment organizer.

holes into the top of the shelf for the brace.

7. Drill countersunk pilot holes in the backside of the back piece for the brace and shelf, and then drill two counterbored pilot holes in the front of the back piece, for mounting your bat organizer.

8. Drill the peg holes all the way through the back piece to match the diameter of the tenon on your pegs.

9. Apply glue to the mating surfaces and screw the shelf and back pieces together. Next, screw the corner brace on.

10. Glue the pegs in place.

References

- Pilot Holes in Chapter 2
- Screw-Hole Plugs in Chapter 2
- Using a Drill in Chapter 2
- Sanding and Finishing in Chapter 5

Tips

- You can make the organizer longer to accommodate more equipment, or simply add pegs to hold more gloves.
- Use a jigsaw instead of a handsaw to cut out the ball and bat-holder holes.
- Before screwing the pieces together, assemble them one at a time and drill a $\frac{1}{8}$-inch pilot hole into the wood through the existing pilot hole to make driving the screws easier and prevent splitting.

CLOCK

This elegant mantel clock (Illus. 6-24–6-26) uses molding to add a special touch.

Tools and Materials Needed

- Handsaw
- Drill
- Miter box
- Brads
- Glue
- Clock mechanism and hands

Illus. 6-24. Clock.

INSTRUCTIONS

1. Cut the parts with a handsaw.

2. Drill dowel holes in the top and bottom of the side pieces centered on the width of the board and $\frac{3}{4}$ inch from the side edges. Next, drill matching holes in the top and bottom pieces, as shown in Fig. 2 of Illus. 6-25.

3. Chamfer the edges of the top piece slightly with a sanding block.

4. Cut miters on the molding using a miter box and glue them to the top and bottom pieces as shown in Figs. 4 and 5 of Illus. 6-26.

5. Install a handle in the top.

6. Tack the front supports to the sides with brads.

7. To assemble the clock, first apply glue to the mating surfaces and in the dowel holes. Then insert the dowels and position the top and bottom onto the sides. Clamp and check the assembly to make sure it is square before allowing it to dry.

8. Drill a hole in the center of the

Cutting List

Part	Qty.	Dimensions	Material
Top	1	$\frac{3}{4}$ x $3\frac{1}{2}$ x 8 inches	Oak
Bottom	1	$\frac{3}{4}$ x $3\frac{1}{2}$ x $7\frac{1}{2}$ inches	Oak
Side	2	$\frac{3}{4}$ x $2\frac{1}{2}$ x 6 inches	Oak
Front	1	$\frac{1}{4}$ x 6 x 6 inches	Oak plywood
Front support	2	$\frac{1}{4}$ x $\frac{1}{2}$ x $4\frac{1}{2}$ inches	Oak plywood
Top molding	4	cut to fit	Oak
Bottom molding	4	cut to fit	Oak

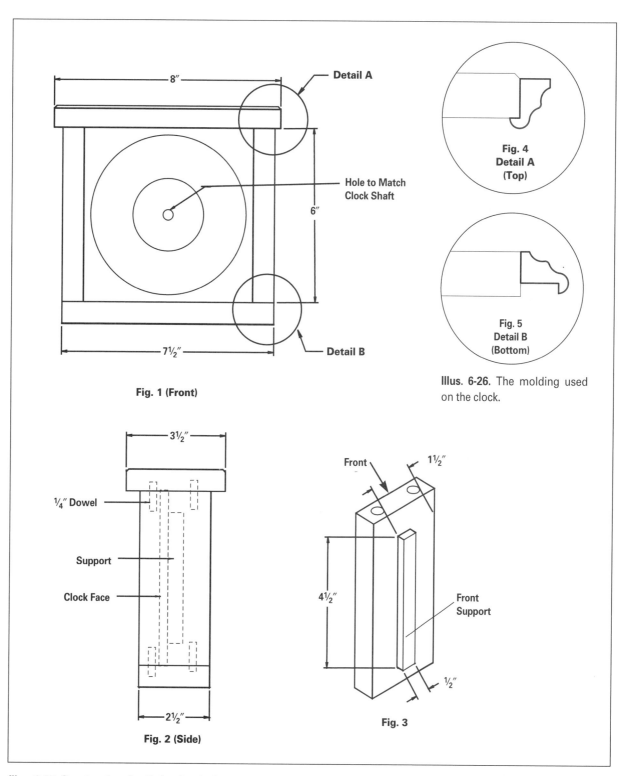

Detail A

**Hole to Match
Clock Shaft**

8″

6″

7½″

Fig. 1 (Front)

Detail B

**Fig. 4
Detail A
(Top)**

**Fig. 5
Detail B
(Bottom)**

Illus. 6-26. The molding used on the clock.

3½″

¼″ Dowel

Support

Clock Face

2½″

Fig. 2 (Side)

Front

1½″

4½″

**Front
Support**

½″

Fig. 3

Illus. 6-25. Construction details for the clock.

Tips

• Instead of using dowels, you can screw the tops and bottoms to the side pieces using counterbored holes and screw-hole plugs.
• When cutting the molding for the top and bottom pieces, cut the pieces out one at a time, measuring each subsequent piece directly from the clock.
• Instead of a sanding block, you can use a hand plane to create the chamfer on the top piece.

plywood clock front to accommodate the diameter of the shaft. Paint the plywood and glue the clock face on. Add the clock mechanism and hands.

9. Glue the plywood face onto the face holder strips and leave it to dry.

References

- Dowels in Chapter 3
- Miter Joints in Chapter 3
- Sanding and Finishing in Chapter 5

CD HOLDER

Keep your favorite compact discs right next to your CD player with this attractive holder (Illus. 6-27 and 6-28). You can expand it simply by making it taller, and, instead of making it freestanding, you can eliminate the base and attach it to a wall.

Tools and Materials Needed

- Handsaw
- Screwdriver
- Drill
- CD case and two business cards

Illus. 6-27. CD holder.

Cutting List

Part	Qty.	Dimensions	Material
Back	1	$\frac{3}{4}$ x $5\frac{1}{2}$ x 14 inches	Maple
Base	1	$\frac{3}{4}$ x $5\frac{1}{2}$ x $6\frac{1}{2}$ inches	Maple
Holder rib	12	$\frac{3}{4}$ x $\frac{3}{4}$ x $5\frac{1}{2}$ inches	Walnut

INSTRUCTIONS

1. Cut the parts with a handsaw.

2. Glue the bottom holder rib exactly $\frac{3}{4}$ inch from the bottom of the back piece and clamp it until it is dry.

3. Place a CD case against the first rib and add two business cards to the top. Glue and clamp the next rib in place. The business cards will ensure there is enough space to easily insert and remove the CD cases. Continue this process, being careful not to shift the previous rib.

4. Allow the complete assembly to dry, and trim the top with a handsaw to match the last rib.

5. To attach the base, drill two countersunk pilot holes into the base $\frac{3}{8}$ inch from the back edge and 1 inch from the sides. Then screw the base to the back. If necessary, drill pilot holes into the back through the pilot holes in the base before screwing the pieces together.

6. For added strength, drill countersunk pilot holes at each rib (Fig. 2 in Illus. 6-28) and screw the back and rib pieces together.

References

• Pilot Holes in Chapter 2
• Sanding and Finishing in Chapter 5

Tips

• You can make this holder any height you want.
• Since the ribs will eventually be screwed on for strength, apply the glue sparingly and allow it to become slightly tacky before putting the rib in place. This will reduce the clamping requirement.
• Have your lumber supplier rip the $\frac{3}{4}$ x $\frac{3}{4}$-inch pieces from a board for you.

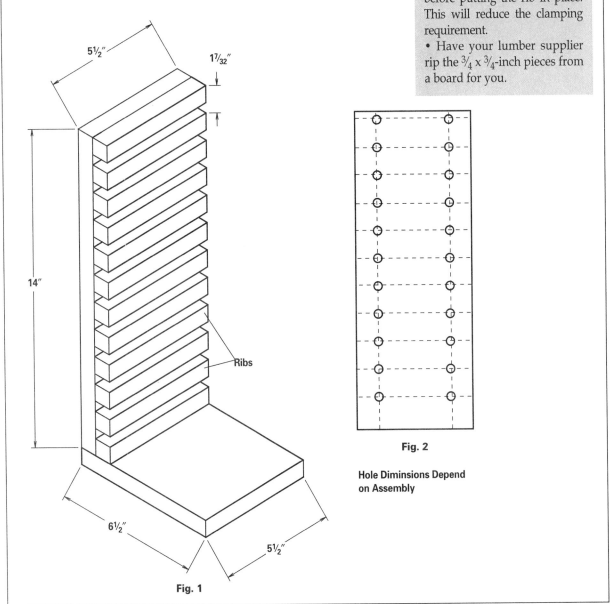

5½"   1⁷/₃₂"

14"

Ribs

6½"   5½"

Fig. 1

Fig. 2

Hole Diminsions Depend on Assembly

Illus. 6-28. Construction details for the CD holder.

MAILBOX

This cedar mailbox (Illus. 6-29 and 6-30) at your front door will make an attractive eye-catcher as well as serve an important function.

Tools and Materials Needed

- Handsaw
- Hammer
- Screwdriver
- Drill
- Hand plane
- Jigsaw
- Piano hinge
- Waterproof glue
- Screws

Illus. 6-29. Mailbox.

Cutting List

Part	Qty.	Dimensions	Material
Back	1	$3/4$ x $5\frac{1}{2}$ x 16 inches	Cedar
Top	1	$3/4$ x $5\frac{1}{2}$ x 19 inches	Cedar
Front	1	$3/4$ x $5\frac{1}{2}$ x 16 inches	Cedar
Bottom	1	$3/4$ x $3\frac{1}{2}$ x 16 inches	Cedar
Side	2	$3/4$ x $5\frac{3}{8}$ x $9\frac{3}{8}$ inches	Cedar

INSTRUCTIONS

1. Cut out the parts with a handsaw.

2. Mark out the side pieces, including the decorative bottom. Make all the straight cuts with a handsaw and use a jigsaw to cut the curves.

3. Use a hand plane to cut the bevel on the bottom piece. This is shown in Fig. 3 of Illus. 6-30.

4. Nail the bottom to the back so the back and ends are flush and the bevel is at the front, facing down.

5. Drill counterbored pilot holes in the side pieces (Fig. 2 in Illus. 6-30), and screw them to the back piece.

6. Drill four counterbored pilot holes evenly spaced along the bottom edge of the front piece $3/8$ inch from the edge. Screw the front piece on so that it is flush with the top and front edge of the side pieces. Next, screw the sides to the front through the screw holes.

7. Screw a piano hinge to the lid and then to the back.

8. Glue screw-hole plugs into the screw holes with waterproof glue.

References

• Using Your Plane in Chapter 2
• Selecting Materials for Outdoor Projects in Chapter 4

Tips

• If you don't have a jigsaw, you can modify the decorative bottom so it only has straight lines that can be cut with a handsaw.
• Add a strip of plastic or rubber under the hinge to act as a weather seal if your mailbox isn't sheltered.

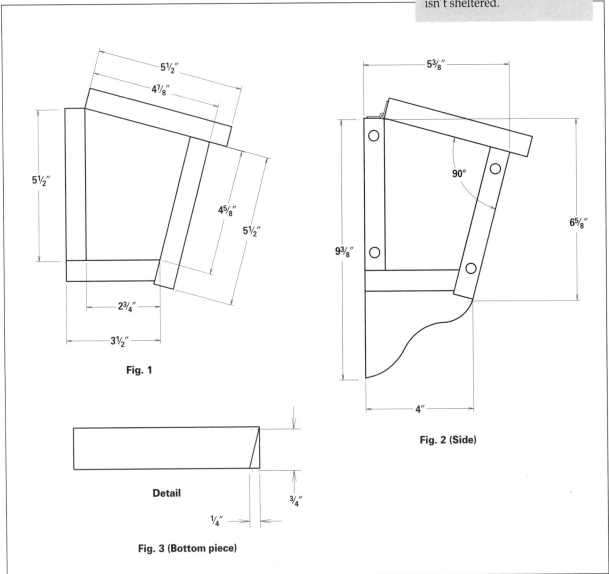

Fig. 1

Fig. 2 (Side)

Detail

Fig. 3 (Bottom piece)

Illus. 6-30. Construction details for the mailbox.

ENTRANCEWAY BENCH

This unique bench (Illus. 6-31 and 6-32) allows you to keep your shoes and boots in the same space as your gloves, hats, scarves, and umbrellas. This project will be a welcome addition not only because it provides for additional storage, but also because it is a place for you or your kids to sit while dressing.

Tools and Materials Needed

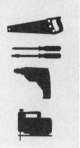

- Handsaw
- Screwdriver
- Drill
- Jigsaw
- Seat hinges
- Screws

INSTRUCTIONS

1. Cut the parts with a handsaw.

2. Use a circle template, compass, or drinking glass to lay out the rounded corners of the seat top, and cut off the waste with a jigsaw. Sand the corner smooth with a sanding block or drum sander mounted in your drill.

3. To make the baseboard cut-out in the sides, drill a $\frac{3}{4}$-inch hole $\frac{3}{8}$ inch in from the back edge of each side piece and $2\frac{5}{8}$ inches up from the bottom, as shown in Fig. 2 of Illus. 6-32. Draw a parallel line from the inside edge of the hole to the bottom; cut this off with a jigsaw or handsaw.

4. Drill counterbored pilot holes in the top rail, back, front, and sides to prepare them for assembly.

5. Drill two $\frac{3}{4}$-inch vent holes in the back 2 inches from the top and each side edge.

6. Screw the sides onto the back so that they are flush at the top.

7. Position the bottom in place so that its lower edge butts up

Illus. 6-31. Entranceway bench.

Cutting List

Part	Qty.	Dimensions	Material
Top rail	1	$\frac{3}{4}$ x $1\frac{1}{2}$ x 24 inches	Pine
Top	1	$\frac{3}{4}$ x 12 x 24 inches	Pine
Side	2	$\frac{3}{4}$ x 12 x $17\frac{1}{4}$ inches	Pine
Front	1	$\frac{3}{4}$ x $7\frac{1}{4}$ x 24 inches	Pine
Back	1	$\frac{3}{4}$ x $7\frac{1}{4}$ x $22\frac{1}{2}$ inches	Pine
Bottom	1	$\frac{3}{4}$ x $11\frac{1}{4}$ x $22\frac{1}{2}$ inches	Plywood

against the back and is exactly $7\frac{1}{4}$ inches from the top of the sides; then screw it in place, as indicated in Fig. 4 of Illus. 6-32.

8. Next, screw the front onto the sides so that it is flush at the front and ends.

9. Assemble the seat top and top

Tips

• You can make the bench longer, to accommodate more items.
• You can use dowels instead of screws.
• If you don't have a jigsaw, you can round the corners on the top with a sanding block and #100 sandpaper.
• Prelaminated panels may not be exactly the size given in the parts list, so take this into consideration and adjust the dimensions as needed.
• Before screwing the pieces together, drill a $\frac{1}{8}$-inch pilot hole into the wood through the existing pilot hole to reduce the possibility of splitting.

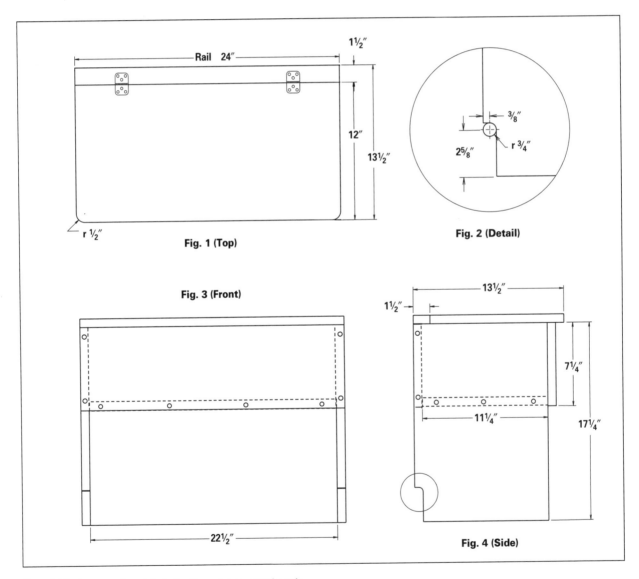

Illus. **6-32.** Construction details for the entranceway bench.

rail together so they are flush at the ends, and screw the seat hinges in place.

10. Put the seat top assembly on the seat assembly and make sure the sides and back are flush before screwing the top rail into the back and side pieces.

References

- Screw-Hole Plugs in Chapter 2
- Pilot Holes in Chapter 2
- Sanding and Finishing in Chapter 5

TOOL CHEST

Make this handsome tool chest (Illus. 6-33–6-35) to store your favorite tools in. You can leave it in one place or take it with you wherever you need it.

Illus. 6-33. Tool chest.

Tools and Materials Needed

• Handsaw
• Screwdriver
• Drill
• Chain
• Brads
• Handle
• Chest hardware

Cutting List

Part	Qty.	Dimensions	Material
Top	2	¾ x 5½ x 18½ inches	Cherry
Lid end	2	¾ x 2½ x 11 inches	Cherry
Box end	2	¾ x 2½ x 11 inches	Cherry
End	2	¾ x 5½ x 11 inches	Cherry
Lid back	1	¾ x 2½ x 20 inches	Cherry
Box back	1	¾ x 2½ x 20 inches	Cherry
Back	1	¾ x 5½ x 20 inches	Cherry
Lid front	1	¾ x 2½ x 20 inches	Cherry
Box front	1	¾ x 2½ x 20 inches	Cherry
Drawer front	1	¾ x 2½ x 20 inches	Walnut
Drawer side	2	¾ x 1½ x 16⅞ inches	Pine
Drawer end	2	¾ x 1½ x 10¾ inches	Pine
Drawer bottom	1	¼ x 18⅜ x 10¾ inches	Plywood
Box bottom	2	½ x 11 x 18½ inches	Plywood
Foot	4	¾ x 2½ x 2½ inches	Walnut

INSTRUCTIONS

1. To make the top, cut two pieces of 5½-inch-wide stock to a length of 19½ inches and glue them together, ensuring that the top surface and one edge are perfectly flush.

2. When the pieces are dry, trim the second edge with a handsaw so the finished piece is exactly 18½ inches long.

3. To make the back of the tool chest, repeat the process with a 5½- and 3½-inch-wide piece cut to an initial length of 21 inches and then trimmed to 20 inches.

4. Do the same for the two ends of the tool chest. Start with 12-inch-long pieces and trim them to 11 inches after gluing them. This length must match the width of the top, so verify the dimensions of the pieces before cutting the two ends, and adjust their length if necessary.

5. Cut the front and back pieces for the lid to a length of 20 inches, and the two lid ends to the same length as the box ends.

rail together so they are flush at the ends, and screw the seat hinges in place.

10. Put the seat top assembly on the seat assembly and make sure the sides and back are flush before screwing the top rail into the back and side pieces.

References

- Screw-Hole Plugs in Chapter 2
- Pilot Holes in Chapter 2
- Sanding and Finishing in Chapter 5

TOOL CHEST

Make this handsome tool chest (Illus. 6-33–6-35) to store your favorite tools in. You can leave it in one place or take it with you wherever you need it.

Illus. 6-33. Tool chest.

Cutting List

Part	Qty.	Dimensions	Material
Top	2	$\frac{3}{4}$ x $5\frac{1}{2}$ x $18\frac{1}{2}$ inches	Cherry
Lid end	2	$\frac{3}{4}$ x $2\frac{1}{2}$ x 11 inches	Cherry
Box end	2	$\frac{3}{4}$ x $2\frac{1}{2}$ x 11 inches	Cherry
End	2	$\frac{3}{4}$ x $5\frac{1}{2}$ x 11 inches	Cherry
Lid back	1	$\frac{3}{4}$ x $2\frac{1}{2}$ x 20 inches	Cherry
Box back	1	$\frac{3}{4}$ x $2\frac{1}{2}$ x 20 inches	Cherry
Back	1	$\frac{3}{4}$ x $5\frac{1}{2}$ x 20 inches	Cherry
Lid front	1	$\frac{3}{4}$ x $2\frac{1}{2}$ x 20 inches	Cherry
Box front	1	$\frac{3}{4}$ x $2\frac{1}{2}$ x 20 inches	Cherry
Drawer front	1	$\frac{3}{4}$ x $2\frac{1}{2}$ x 20 inches	Walnut
Drawer side	2	$\frac{3}{4}$ x $1\frac{1}{2}$ x $16\frac{7}{8}$ inches	Pine
Drawer end	2	$\frac{3}{4}$ x $1\frac{1}{2}$ x $10\frac{3}{4}$ inches	Pine
Drawer bottom	1	$\frac{1}{4}$ x $18\frac{3}{8}$ x $10\frac{3}{4}$ inches	Plywood
Box bottom	2	$\frac{1}{2}$ x 11 x $18\frac{1}{2}$ inches	Plywood
Foot	4	$\frac{3}{4}$ x $2\frac{1}{2}$ x $2\frac{1}{2}$ inches	Walnut

Tools and Materials Needed

- Handsaw
- Screwdriver
- Drill
- Chain
- Brads
- Handle
- Chest hardware

INSTRUCTIONS

1. To make the top, cut two pieces of $5\frac{1}{2}$-inch-wide stock to a length of $19\frac{1}{2}$ inches and glue them together, ensuring that the top surface and one edge are perfectly flush.

2. When the pieces are dry, trim the second edge with a handsaw so the finished piece is exactly $18\frac{1}{2}$ inches long.

3. To make the back of the tool chest, repeat the process with a $5\frac{1}{2}$- and $3\frac{1}{2}$-inch-wide piece cut to an initial length of 21 inches and then trimmed to 20 inches.

4. Do the same for the two ends of the tool chest. Start with 12-inch-long pieces and trim them to 11 inches after gluing them. This length must match the width of the top, so verify the dimensions of the pieces before cutting the two ends, and adjust their length if necessary.

5. Cut the front and back pieces for the lid to a length of 20 inches, and the two lid ends to the same length as the box ends.

6. To assemble the lid, butt the front piece and one end piece together and drill two countersunk pilot holes $\frac{3}{8}$ inch from the end of the front and $\frac{3}{4}$ inch from each piece. Clamp the pieces together before drilling the pilot holes, to make sure you

have an accurate, flush assembly. Apply glue and screw the pieces together.

7. Position the top piece inside this assembly so that it is flush with

Illus. **6-34.** This tool chest has plenty of space for tools.

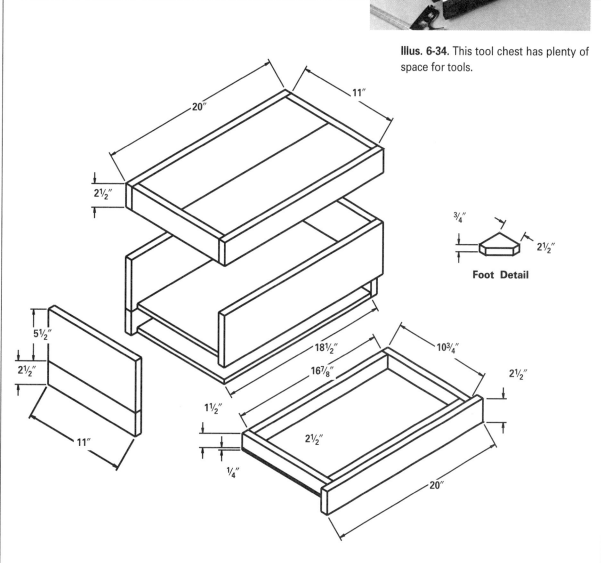

Illus. **6-35.** Construction details for the tool chest.

the top edges. Drill countersunk pilot holes along the front and end pieces $\frac{3}{8}$ inch from the top edge. Apply glue and screw the pieces together.

8. Add the second side and the back of the lid using the same process.

9. For the box, use the same process as for the lid, ensuring that the box ends up with the same dimensions as the lid. First assemble the front and one end, and then add the second end, ensuring they are flush at their top edges. Add the bottom so that it is flush with the bottom of the front piece. Finally, add the back.

10. To make the drawer, drill two countersunk pilot holes $\frac{3}{8}$ inch in from the ends of the drawer

sides and screw the sides to the front and back pieces. Glue the bottom of the drawer in place and tack it on with brads.

11. Screw the drawer front to the drawer assembly from the inside through two countersunk pilot holes so that it is flush at the top and centered side to side.

12. Turn the box upside down and lay the drawer, also upside down, in place. Place two business cards or other thick paper in each corner and add the bottom. Drill countersunk pilot holes into the bottom from the sides and back of the chest. Then apply glue and screw the bottom in place.

13. Attach the chest hardware to the front and a handle on each side.

A chain should be attached to the inside of the box and box lid to prevent the lid from opening completely.

14. Cut out the four feet and drill countersunk pilot holes in them. Screw them to the bottom at the corners.

Tips

• You can use dowels instead of screws to hold the box and lid together.
• If you use cut brass screws, you have to drill a clearance hole for the shank.

References

• Pilot Holes in Chapter 2
• Sanding and Finishing in Chapter 5

TOOLBOX

This simple, traditional toolbox (Illus. 6-36 and 6-37) will hold all the tools you need and makes it easy for you to bring your tools to the work.

Tools and Materials Needed

- Handsaw
- Screwdriver
- Drill
- Jigsaw

Illus. 6-36. Tool box.

Cutting List

Part	Qty.	Dimensions	Material
Side	2	$\frac{3}{4}$ x $7\frac{1}{4}$ x 20 inches	Pine
Bottom	1	$\frac{3}{4}$ x $7\frac{1}{4}$ x 20 inches	Pine
End	2	$\frac{3}{4}$ x $7\frac{1}{4}$ x 11 inches	Pine
Handle support	2	$\frac{3}{4}$ x $2\frac{1}{2}$ x 12 inches	Pine
Handle	1	$1\frac{1}{4}$-inch-diameter dowel	Maple

INSTRUCTIONS

1. Cut out the parts with a handsaw.

2. On each end piece, measure $1\frac{1}{8}$ inches in from the ends at the bottom. Extend this point to the top corner; then cut off the waste with a handsaw.

3. Drill countersunk pilot holes in the end pieces $\frac{3}{8}$ inch in from the bottom and sides.

4. Holding one end up, position a side piece so that it is flush with the end piece at its edge and top; then screw the end piece to the side piece through the pilot holes.

5. Repeat this step for the second side and the bottom.

6. Position the second end against the assembly and screw it on, making sure its bottom and sides are flush.

7. Mark the center for the handle on both handle supports, and

draw its outer radius with a compass.

8. Cut along the line with a jigsaw. Sand the edge smooth.

9. Drill a hole for the handle in each handle support with a 1¼-inch hole saw mounted in your drill. Make sure you drill the hole straight and use a backing board to reduce tear-out.

10. Position a handle support inside one end of the tool box so that it is centered side to side and butts up against the bottom, and then screw it in place. Repeat this for the second handle support.

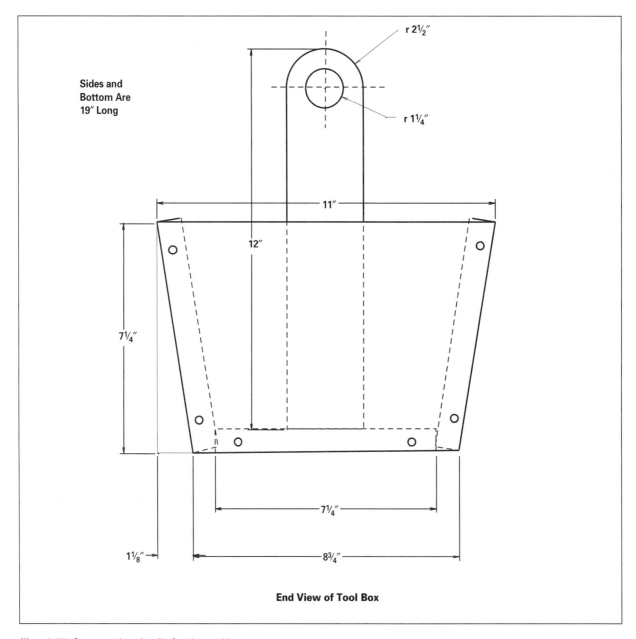

Illus. 6-37. Construction details for the tool box.

11. Insert the handle into the handle support so that it extends past the support the same amount on each end.

12. Drill a countersunk pilot hole through one handle support into the handle.

13. Drive a screw through the handle support and into the handle through the pilot hole you just drilled. This will keep the handle from twisting in use.

References

• Pilot Holes in Chapter 2
• Using a Drill in Chapter 2

Tips

• If you leave the top of the handle supports square, you won't need a jigsaw.
• Drill a $\frac{1}{8}$-inch pilot hole into the wood through the existing pilot hole before screwing the pieces together, to reduce the chance of splitting.

WINDOW PLANTER

Dress up your windowsill by displaying your favorite flowers in this cedar planter (Illus. 6-38 and 6-39). As an alternative, you can even hang it from your balcony or patio railing.

Tools and Materials Needed

- Handsaw
- Hammer
- Nails
- Hand plane

INSTRUCTIONS

1. Cut out the parts with a handsaw.

2. On each of the end pieces, measure $3\frac{1}{2}$ inches along its bottom edge and make a mark (Fig. 1 in Illus. 6-39). Extend this mark to the top corner of the piece, and cut off the waste with a handsaw.

3. Cut a bevel with your hand plane on the bottom piece to match the end pieces (Fig. 2 in Illus. 6-39).

4. On one of the front pieces, measure $\frac{3}{4}$ inch in from each edge, and then make a mark every two inches. Connect the marks at right angles, as shown in Fig. 3 in Illus. 6-39, and cut out the waste with a handsaw.

5. Assemble the bottom, back, and end pieces to mark the location where the back meets the end pieces. Then draw a 45-degree mark to extend this point to the top of the end piece. Cut out the waste with a jigsaw.

6. Nail the bottom piece to the back piece with nails spaced 4

Illus. 6-38. Window planter.

Cutting List

Part	Qty.	Dimensions	Material
Back	1	$\frac{3}{4} \times 5\frac{1}{2} \times 31\frac{1}{2}$ inches	Cedar
Bottom	1	$\frac{3}{4} \times 3\frac{1}{2} \times 31\frac{1}{2}$ inches	Cedar
Front	2	$\frac{3}{4} \times 3\frac{1}{2} \times 31\frac{1}{2}$ inches	Cedar
End	2	$\frac{3}{4} \times 5\frac{1}{2} \times 5$ inches	Cedar

inches apart, making sure the bottom piece's bevel matches the end pieces. Add the end pieces so they are inset about ½ inch in and nail them on from the back and bottom of the assembly.

7. Lay this assembly on its back and add the bottom front piece, lining up its bottom edges. Nail this onto the bottom and end pieces. Add the top front piece, nailing it to the ends only.

References

• Using Your Plane in Chapter 2
• Selecting Materials for Outdoor Projects in Chapter 4

Tips

• You can create a different design on the front edge, especially if you have a jigsaw.
• Drill a pilot hole for the nails, to reduce the chance of splitting the wood.

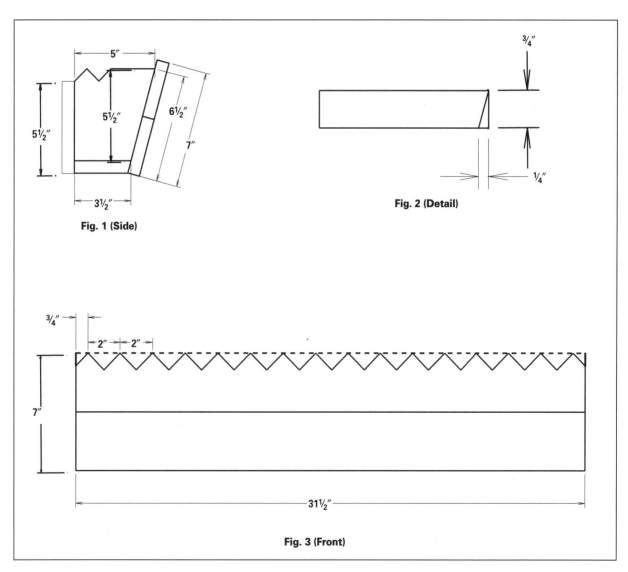

Fig. 1 (Side)

Fig. 2 (Detail)

Fig. 3 (Front)

Illus. 6-39. Construction details for the window planter.

FIREWOOD BOX

With this firewood box (Illus. 6-40 and 6-41), you can keep a supply of firewood, kindling, and newspapers close at hand to light your fire, and then refill the box with wood from your wood pile whenever it's convenient.

Tools and Materials Needed

- Handsaw
- Hammer
- Screwdriver
- Drill
- Hand plane
- Hinges
- Handle
- Brads
- Screw-hole plugs
- Screws

Illus. 6-40. Firewood box.

INSTRUCTIONS

1. Cut out the parts with a handsaw.

2. On both side panels, measure for the angled cut $5\frac{5}{8}$ inches from the back on the top edge and $18\frac{15}{16}$ inches from the bottom on the front edge.

3. Use a framing square or straight piece of wood to draw a line between the marks and saw the waste off, keeping to the outside of the lines.

4. Use a sanding block or a hand plane to smooth the cut edges.

5. Several bevels have to be cut in the lid, front, and top panels, so mark both edges of the lid, one edge of the front panel, and one edge of the top panel. The bevel detail is shown in Fig. 2 of Illus. 6-42.

6. Drill counterbored pilot holes in the side panels along the edges where the back, front, and top

Cutting List

Part	Qty.	Dimensions	Material
Side panel	2	$\frac{3}{4}$ x $15\frac{3}{4}$ x $28\frac{1}{2}$ inches	Pine
Front panel	1	$\frac{3}{4}$ x $15\frac{3}{4}$ x 22 inches	Pine
Lid	1	$\frac{3}{4}$ x $11\frac{3}{4}$ x $21\frac{7}{8}$ inches	Pine
Top panel	1	$\frac{3}{4}$ x $5\frac{1}{2}$ x $23\frac{3}{4}$ inches	Pine
Back panel	1	$\frac{1}{2}$ x 22 x $28\frac{1}{2}$ inches	Plywood
Bottom panel	1	$\frac{1}{2}$ x $14\frac{1}{4}$ x $23\frac{3}{4}$ inches	Plywood
Drawer face	1	$\frac{3}{4}$ x $5\frac{1}{2}$ x $23\frac{5}{8}$ inches	Pine
Drawer side	2	$\frac{3}{4}$ x $3\frac{1}{2}$ x $12\frac{1}{2}$ inches	Pine
Drawer front/back	2	$\frac{3}{4}$ x $3\frac{1}{2}$ x $22\frac{3}{4}$ inches	Pine
Drawer bottom	1	$\frac{1}{4}$ x 14 x $22\frac{3}{4}$ inches	Plywood

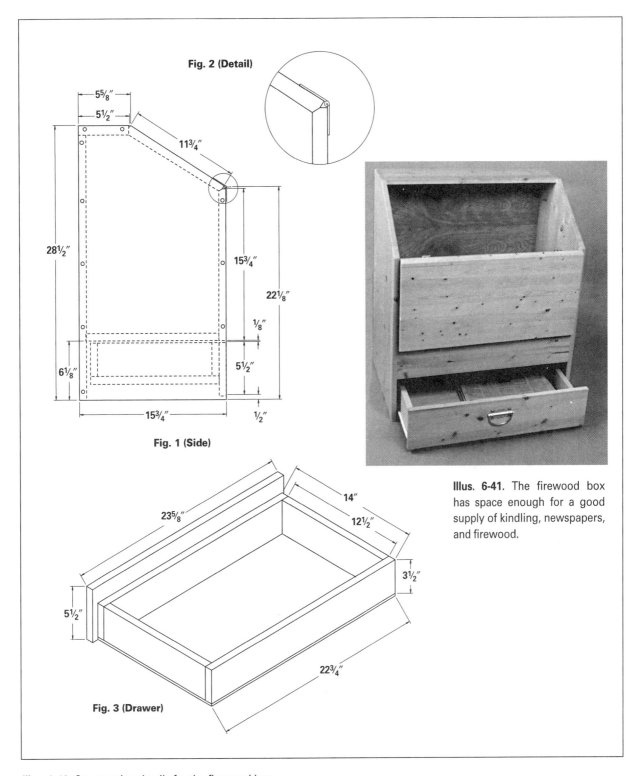

Fig. 2 (Detail)

5⁵⁄₈″

5¹⁄₂″

11³⁄₄″

28¹⁄₂″

15³⁄₄″

22¹⁄₈″

¹⁄₈″

5¹⁄₂″

6¹⁄₈″

15³⁄₄″

¹⁄₂″

Fig. 1 (Side)

23⁵⁄₈″

14″

12¹⁄₂″

3¹⁄₂″

5¹⁄₂″

22³⁄₄″

Fig. 3 (Drawer)

Illus. 6-41. The firewood box has space enough for a good supply of kindling, newspapers, and firewood.

Illus. 6-42. Construction details for the firewood box.

pieces will be attached, as shown in Fig. 1 of Illus. 6-42.

7. Apply glue and screw the side panels to the back, bottom, top, and front panels. Check that the box is square, and allow it to dry.

8. Attach the hinges and handle to the door, position it on the box, and screw the hinges onto the box.

9. Drill countersunk pilot holes in the ends of the front and back drawer pieces $\frac{3}{8}$ inch from the end and $\frac{1}{2}$ inch from each edge.

10. Screw the back and front pieces onto the sides so that they are flush at the ends and on top. Glue and tack the drawer bottom in place with brads.

11. Add the handle to the drawer face, and then screw it to the drawer through countersunk pilot holes from inside the drawer, so that it is centered side to side and flush at the top.

12. Install the drawer guides, following the instructions they come with.

13. Glue screw-hole plugs into the screw holes.

Tips

• Not all prelaminated panels are exactly the same width, so adjust the measurements of the panels as required, to ensure they are uniform.
• Before screwing the pieces together, drill a $\frac{1}{8}$-inch pilot hole into the wood through the existing pilot hole to reduce the possibility of splintering.
• You can use dowels instead of screws.

References

• Using a Plane in Chapter 2
• Screw-Hole Plugs in Chapter 2
• Pilot Holes in Chapter 2
• Sanding and Finishing in Chapter 5

CHILDREN'S TABLE

This unique table (Illus. 6-43–6-47) solves the problem of what to do with your children's art supplies. Simply flip up the top and you have lots of storage space for coloring books, crayons, and everything else.

Tools and Materials Needed

- Handsaw
- Screwdriver
- Drill
- Sanding block or hand plane
- Hinges
- Chain

Illus. 6-43. Children's table.

Cutting List

Part	Qty.	Dimensions	Material
Tabletop	1	³/₄ x 19³/₄ x 35³/₄ inches	Pine
Table skirt	2	³/₄ x 3¹/₂ x 18¹/₄ inches	Pine
Table skirt	2	³/₄ x 3¹/₂ x 32³/₄ inches	Pine
Leg piece (A)	4	³/₄ x 2¹/₄ x 19¹/₂ inches	Pine
Leg piece (B)	4	³/₄ x 1¹/₂ x 19¹/₂ inches	Pine
Leg Piece (C)	4	³/₄ x ³/₄ x 16 inches	Pine
Leg piece (D)	4	³/₄ x 1¹/₂ x 16 inches	Pine
Shelf support	4	³/₄ x ³/₄ x 15 inches	Pine
Shelf	1	¹/₂ x 16⁵/₈ x 32⁵/₈ inches	Plywood

INSTRUCTIONS

1. Cut out all the parts with the exception of the legs.

2. For the legs, rip a 2¹/₄-inch-wide piece from a 3¹/₂-inch-wide board, and then smooth the edge with a sanding block or hand plane.

3. Assemble and glue the leg pieces (Fig. 1 in Illus. 6-44). To ensure the correct offset between the short and long pieces, use a scrap piece of 3¹/₂-inch board as a guide. It may be easier to glue the leg pieces together one at a time, waiting for each one to dry before adding the next.

4. Drill countersunk pilot holes in the ends and middle of each ledge piece and screw them to the inside of the table skirt pieces so they are flush with the bottom and centered from end to end (Fig. 2 in Illus. 6-44).

5. Drill countersunk pilot holes in the skirt end pieces ¹/₂ inch from the ends and ¹/₂ inch from the top and bottom edges. Apply

113

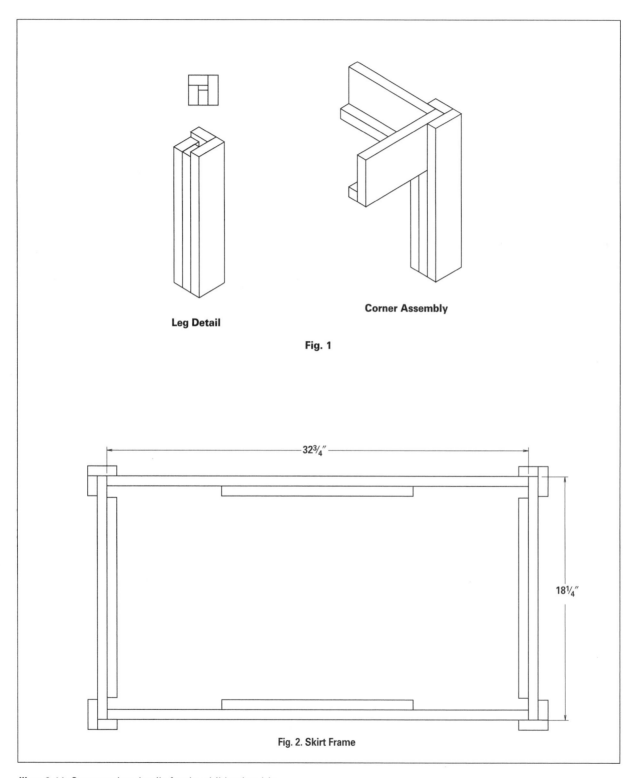

Leg Detail

Corner Assembly

Fig. 1

32³⁄₄″

18¹⁄₄″

Fig. 2. Skirt Frame

Illus. 6-44. Construction details for the children's table.

glue to the mating surfaces and screw the skirts to the leg pieces from the inside so that they are flush with the top and butting up against the leg pieces.

6. Drill countersunk pilot holes in the front and back skirt pieces $\frac{3}{8}$ inch from the ends and $\frac{1}{2}$ inch from the top and bottom edges. Apply glue to the mating surfaces and screw the skirts to the

leg pieces from the inside flush with the top and butting up against the end skirt pieces.

7. Insert the bottom of the table into the frame made by the table skirts and screw it in place from below through the ledge with one screw on each side.

8. Screw the hinges to the underside of the long side of the table-

top 2 inches from each end so that they line up with the legs. Place the tabletop onto the table and screw the hinges into the legs. The width of the hinges should be less than the width of the legs (Fig. 4 in Illus. 6-46).

9. Install a chain at both sides to keep the tabletop from being opened too far. If desired, use a lid closer for safety.

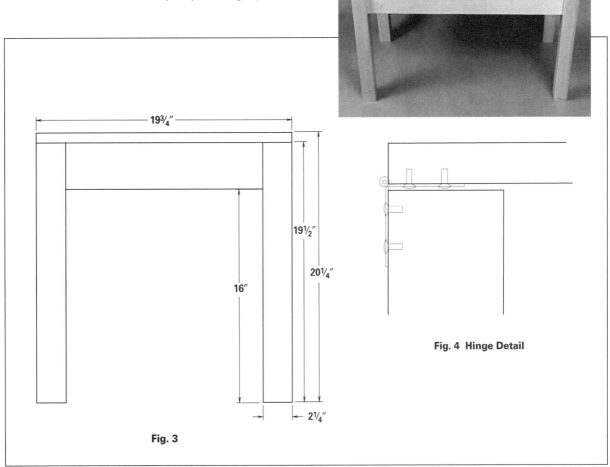

Illus. 6-45. When you flip up the top of this table, you'll find plenty of storage space.

Fig. 4 Hinge Detail

Fig. 3

Illus. 6-46. Construction details for the children's table.

Tips

• You can glue up your own panel for the tabletop.
• You can have the 2¼-inch leg pieces ripped for you at your lumber supply store.

References

• Pilot Holes in Chapter 2
• Using Your Handsaw in Chapter 2
• Sanding and Finishing in Chapter 5

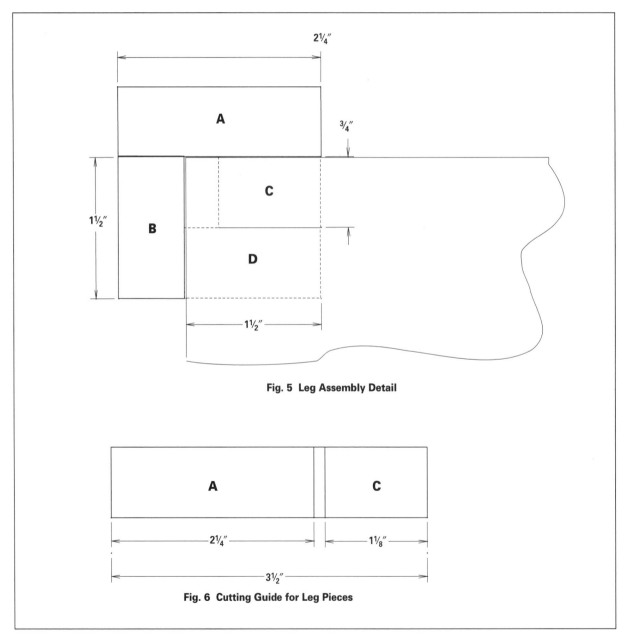

Fig. 5 Leg Assembly Detail

Fig. 6 Cutting Guide for Leg Pieces

Illus. 6-47. Construction details for the children's table.

CHILDREN'S CHAIR

A good companion for the children's table, this chair (Illus. 6-48 and 6-49) is sturdy and easy to build.

Tools and Materials Needed

- Handsaw
- Screwdriver
- Drill
- Sandpaper
- Dowels
- Screw-hole plugs

Illus. 6-48. Children's chair.

INSTRUCTIONS

1. Cut out the parts with a handsaw.

2. Lightly round all corners and edges with a piece of folded #180 sandpaper.

3. Drill the dowel holes in the side rails as shown in Figs. 1 and 2 of Illus. 6-49.

4. Drill matching holes in the front and back legs as shown in Figs. 1 and 2 of Illus. 6-49.

5. Apply glue to the dowels and insert them into the side rails; then apply glue to the end of the side rails and assemble the front and back legs and the side rails to make the chair sides. Clamp the assembly together, making sure the legs are parallel and square to the side rail.

6. Once the assembly is dry, drill counterbored pilot holes for the crosspieces in each chair side, as shown in Fig. 2 of Illus. 6-49.

7. Apply glue and screw the two crosspieces for the seat in place.

8. Drill one countersunk pilot

Cutting List

Part	Qty.	Dimensions	Material
Front leg	2	¾ x 1½ x 11 inches	Pine
Back leg	2	¾ x 1½ x 22 inches	Pine
Side rail	2	¾ x 1½ x 8 inches	Pine
Crosspiece	4	¾ x 1½ x 10¾ inches	Pine
Seat slat	6	¾ x 1½ x 11 inches	Pine

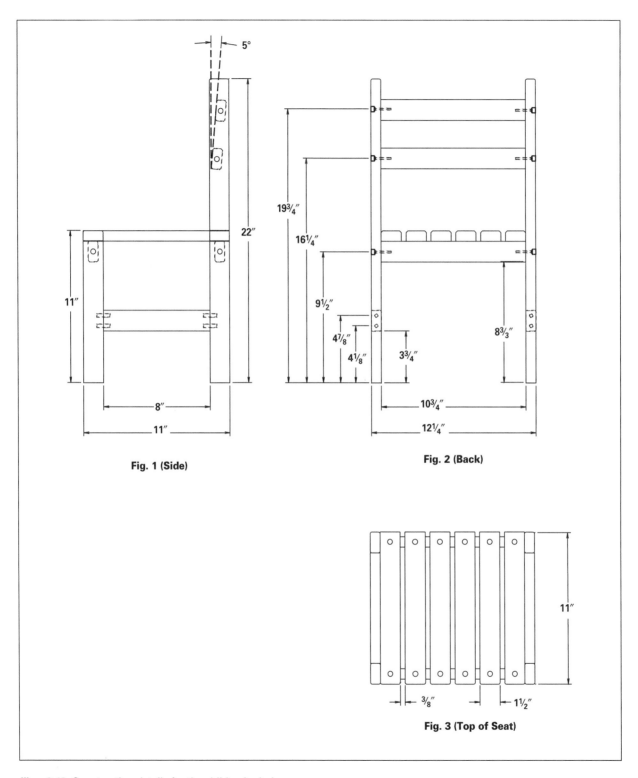

Fig. 1 (Side)

Fig. 2 (Back)

Fig. 3 (Top of Seat)

Illus. 6-49. Construction details for the children's chair.

hole $\frac{3}{8}$ inch from each end of the seat slats as shown in Fig. 3 of Illus. 6-49.

9. Apply glue to the mating surfaces, and screw the seat slats to

the crosspieces so that the slats are flush with the front and evenly spaced.

10. Apply glue to the mating surfaces and screw the cross-

pieces for the seat back in place at the angle shown in Fig. 1 of Illus. 6-49.

11. Glue flat screw-hole plugs in place.

Tips

• Instead of using dowels for the side rails, you can drill deep counter-bored pilot holes and screw the pieces together.
• Drill $\frac{1}{8}$-inch pilot holes in the center of the ends of each crosspiece for easy alignment when screwing them in place.

References

• Pilot Holes in Chapter 2
• Screw-Hole Plugs in Chapter 2
• Dowels in Chapter 3
• Sanding and Finishing in Chapter 5

GARDEN TRAY

Use this gardening tray (Illus. 6-50 and 6-51) to keep your gardening tools and supplies portable and close at hand while tending your garden.

Tools and Materials Needed

• Handsaw
• Hammer
• Drill
• Jigsaw
• Sanding block or plane
• Nails

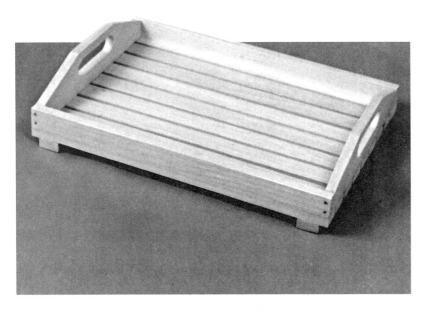

Illus. 6-50. Garden tray.

Cutting List

Part	Qty.	Dimensions	Material
Bottom and cross slat	11	$3/4$ x $1^1/_2$ x $23^3/_4$ inches	Pine
Cross slat	2	$3/4$ x $1^1/_2$ x $17^1/_2$ inches	Pine
Handle	2	$3/4$ x $3^1/_2$ x 16 inches	Pine

Tips

• Use screws instead of nails to assemble the garden tray.
• Drill pilot holes for the nails, to reduce the chances of splintering.

INSTRUCTIONS

1. Cut out the parts with a handsaw.

2. Lay the nine slats for the bottom down on your workbench flush at their ends with approximately a $1/2$-inch gap between each one of them so they end up with a total width of $17^1/_2$ inches.

3. Lay the two cross slats on top of the bottom slats at each end so they are inset 1 inch from the ends of the bottom slats and flush at their edges. Nail the cross slats onto each bottom slat with two $1^1/_4$-inch nails where each slat crosses.

4. Turn the bottom over and position it over two side slats so they are flush at the sides and ends. Nail them in place with at least six nails.

5. To make the handles, first measure 2 inches down and $3^1/_2$ inches in at each end of the handle pieces. Join these marks with a ruler and cut the waste off with a handsaw, cleaning up the cut edge with a sanding block or plane.

6. Mark the centers of the holes as shown in Fig. 2 of Illus. 6-51 and drill them out, using a backing board to reduce splintering.

7. To make the handle opening, join the top and bottom edges of the circles with a straight line and cut along the line with a jigsaw.

8. Position the handles on the tray and nail them in from the sides with two nails at each end.

9. Flip the tray over and drive one 2½-inch nail through each slat into the handles.

References

• Using a Drill in Chapter 2

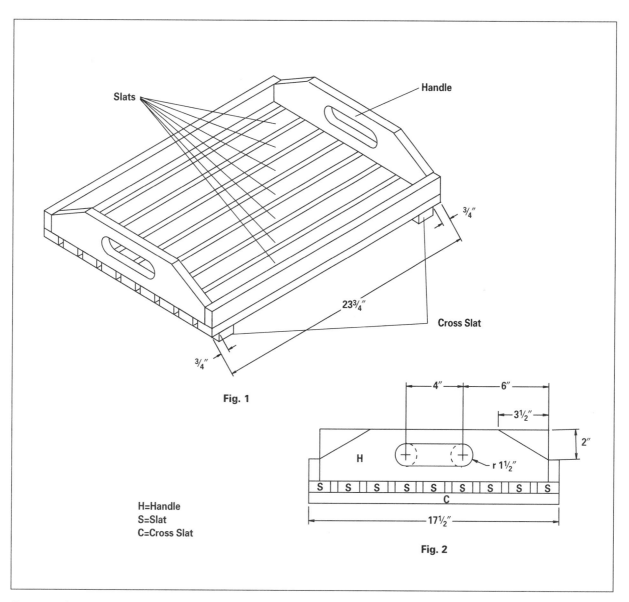

Fig. 1

H=Handle
S=Slat
C=Cross Slat

Fig. 2

Illus. **6-51.** Construction details for the garden tray.

CUTTING BOARDS

An attractive wooden cutting board (Illus. 6-52–6-54) is not only a pleasure to use, it can also be a good way to use up shorter scraps of hardwood. Build these two versions or create your own. You can make a small version for cutting up an occasional onion, and a larger one for creating a meal.

Tools and Materials Needed

- Handsaw
- Square or ruler
- Sanding block
- Mineral oil

CUTTING BOARD #1

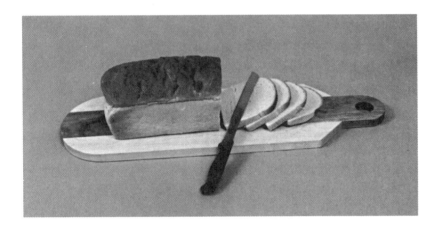

Illus. 6-52. Cutting board.

Cutting List for Board #1

Part	Qty.	Dimensions	Material
End board	2	$3/4$ x $2^1/_2$ x $23^1/_2$ inches	Hardwood
Middle board	1	$3/4$ x $3^1/_2$ x 27 inches	Hardwood

Tips

- You can make the cutting board as long or as wide as you want.
- After gluing up the panel, you can use a hand plane instead of a sanding block to smooth the top of the cutting board.

INSTRUCTIONS FOR CUTTING BOARD #1

1. Cut the parts with a handsaw.

2. Glue up the boards so that one end and the top surfaces are perfectly flush.

3. When the board is dry, use a square or ruler to mark a line along the edge that isn't flush and cut it off.

4. Measure down $2^1/_2$ inches along the side on each end and join this point with the joint between the end board and the next board. Cut the corner off with a handsaw.

5. Sand or plane the edge smooth.

6. Sand the entire board with a sanding block or hand plane, rounding the edges slightly.

7. Apply a liberal coat of mineral oil, allow it to soak in for several hours, and wipe it off. Repeat this regularly after every couple of months of use.

Reference

- Gluing Up Boards in Chapter 3

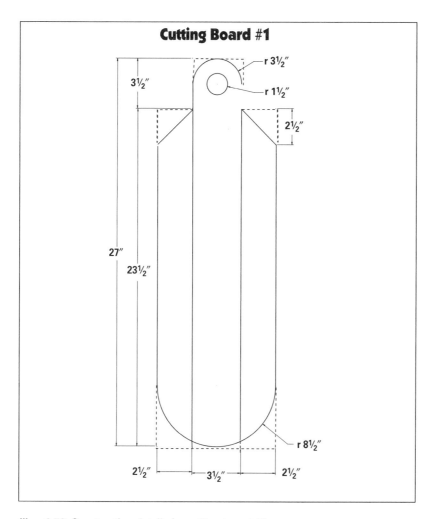

Cutting Board #1

r 3½"

3½"

r 1½"

2½"

27"

23½"

r 8½"

2½"   3½"   2½"

Illus. 6-53. Construction details for cutting board #1.

Cutting List for board #2

Part	Qty.	Dimensions	Material
Middle board	2	¾ x 1½ x 14½ inches	Hardwood
Side board	3	¾ x 2½ x 14½ inches	Hardwood

Tips

• You can cut out the handle with a jigsaw if you want smooth, flowing curves.
• After gluing up the panel, you can use a hand plane instead of a sanding block to smooth the top of the cutting board.

CUTTING BOARD #2

Tools and Materials Needed

• Handsaw
• Drill
• Sanding block or hand plane
• Compass
• Jigsaw
• Mineral oil

INSTRUCTIONS FOR CUTTING BOARD #2

1. Cut the parts with a handsaw.

2. Measure 2½ inches down one side of each of the 2½-inch-wide boards. Join this point with the corner on the other board, making a 45-degree angle. Cut off the corner with a handsaw and smooth the cut edge with a sanding block or hand plane.

3. Glue up the boards so that the tips of the two side boards are offset 3½ inches from one end of the middle board.

4. When the boards are dry, use a compass to draw a circle at both ends of them, and cut off the waste with a jigsaw. Sand the edges smooth with a sanding block or drum sander mounted in your drill.

5. Drill a 1½-inch hole in the handle end with a hole saw, using a backing board to prevent splintering.

6. Sand the entire board with a sanding block, rounding the edges slightly.

7. Apply a liberal coat of mineral oil. Allow it to soak in for several hours, and then wipe it off. Repeat this regularly after every couple of months of use.

References

• Gluing Up Boards in Chapter 3

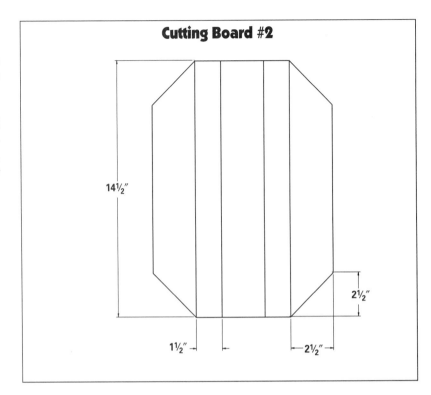

Illus. 6-54. Construction details for cutting board #2.

GARDEN BENCH

This easy-to-make garden bench (Illus. 6-56 and 6-57) is the perfect place to sit, relax, and enjoy your yard or garden.

Tools and Materials Needed

- Handsaw
- Drill
- Screws
- #100 sandpaper

Illus. 6-55. Garden bench.

Cutting List

Part	Qty.	Dimensions	Material
Back slat (E)	2	$1\frac{1}{2}$ x $7\frac{1}{4}$ x 48 inches	Cedar
Seat slat (C)	2	$1\frac{1}{2}$ x $7\frac{1}{4}$ x 48 inches	Cedar
Seat front ledge (B)	1	$1\frac{1}{2}$ x $5\frac{1}{2}$ x 48 inches	Cedar
Back top (F)	1	$1\frac{1}{2}$ x $3\frac{1}{2}$ x 48 inches	Cedar
Back support (G)	2	$1\frac{1}{2}$ x $3\frac{1}{2}$ x $34\frac{3}{4}$ inches	Cedar
Seat support (D)	2	$1\frac{1}{2}$ x $3\frac{1}{2}$ x 16 inches	Cedar
Front support (A)	2	$1\frac{1}{2}$ x $3\frac{1}{2}$ x 16 inches	Cedar
Bottom support (H)	2	$1\frac{1}{2}$ x $3\frac{1}{2}$ x 24 inches	Cedar

INSTRUCTIONS

1. Cut out the parts.

2. On the bottom supports, measure 2 inches from an edge along one end, and mark a 45-degree line from this point. Cut off the corner by sawing to the outside of this line (Fig. 1 in Illus. 6-56).

3. On one end of both the back and seat supports, measure 1 inch along an edge from the end and join this mark with the opposite corner. Cut off the corners by sawing to the outside of this line (Fig. 2 in Illus. 6-56).

4. Position all the pieces for each end together, with the front and back supports on top of the seat and bottom supports. Make certain the two sides are mirror images of each other, and screw them together with two $2\frac{1}{2}$-inch screws where each piece crosses.

5. Set the ends upright so the screw heads are facing inward and screw the seat front ledge onto the front of the side pieces with two screws on each end so

125

that it overhangs at the ends by 2 inches.

6. Screw the first seat slat on, flush at the front and overhanging by 2 inches at the ends. Leave a $\frac{1}{4}$-inch gap and screw the second seat slat on.

7. Screw the top piece in place, allowing it to overhang by 2 inches on each end.

8. Position the top back slat in place flush at the top and over-hanging by 2 inches at the ends, and then screw it in place. Leave a 1-inch gap, position the sec-ond back slat in place, and screw it on.

9. Sand all the edges of the boards smooth with #100 sandpaper.

References

• Selecting Materials for Outdoor Projects in Chapter 4

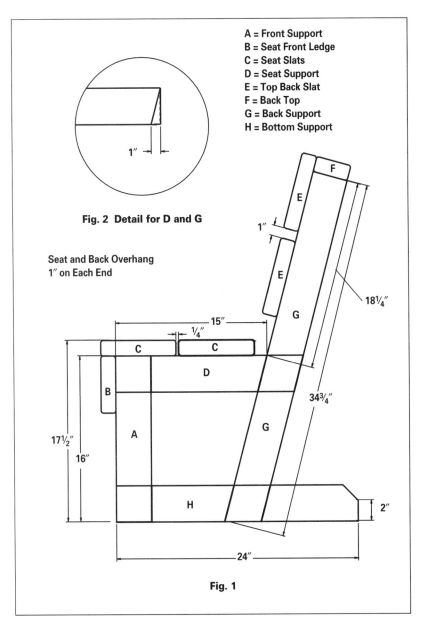

Illus. 6-56. Construction details for the garden bench.

Tips

• You can make this seat longer or shorter than the illustrations indicate, if desired.
• For this project, use your drill and power-driver bits to drive the screws.
• Drill countersunk pilot holes for easy assembly and to reduce splintering.

GARDEN PLANTER

This easy-to-make cedar planter (Illus. 6-57 and 6-58) is great for any yard, patio, or balcony. It can be used for shrubs, flowers, herbs, or even garden vegetables such as tomatoes.

Tools and Materials Needed

- Handsaw
- Hammer
- Nails

Illus. 6-57. Garden planter.

Cutting List

Part	Qty.	Dimensions	Material
Vertical piece	16	$3/4 \times 3\frac{1}{2} \times 16$ inches	Cedar
Short end rail	2	$3/4 \times 3\frac{1}{2} \times 14$ inches	Cedar
Long end rail	2	$3/4 \times 3\frac{1}{2} \times 17$ inches	Cedar
Short bottom ledge	2	$3/4 \times 1\frac{1}{2} \times 12\frac{1}{2}$ inches	Cedar
Long bottom ledge	2	$3/4 \times 1\frac{1}{2} \times 14$ inches	Cedar
Bottom piece	4	$3/4 \times 3\frac{1}{2} \times 14$ inches	Cedar

INSTRUCTIONS

1. Cut out the parts with a handsaw.

2. To make the sides, lay four vertical pieces side by side so their ends line up. Lay a long bottom ledge over these pieces, flush at each end and extending beyond the vertical pieces by $1\frac{1}{2}$ inches. Nail the ledge to the vertical piece with two $1\frac{1}{4}$-inch nails where each vertical piece overlaps.

3. Lift the opposite end of the side and slide a short end rail underneath, positioning it flush at the top and sides. Nail it on with two nails where each vertical piece overlaps.

4. Repeat steps 2 and 3 for the second side.

5. To make the ends, lay four vertical pieces side by side so their ends line up. Lay a short bottom ledge over these, centered from side to side, and extending $1\frac{1}{2}$ inches at each end and beyond the vertical pieces by $1\frac{1}{2}$ inches. Nail the ledge to the vertical piece with two nails where each vertical piece overlaps.

127

6. Lift the opposite end and slide a long end rail underneath it, positioning it flush at the top and so it extends 1½ inches at each end. Nail it on with two nails where each vertical piece overlaps.

7. Repeat steps 5 and 6 for the second side.

8. Assemble the four pieces and nail their corners together.

9. Place the bottom pieces inside the planter so they rest on the ledges.

Reference

• Selecting Materials for Outdoor Projects in Chapter 4

Tips

• You can make the planter longer or larger by lengthening or adding vertical pieces.
• The measurements given in Illus. 6-58 rely on your boards being exactly the standard size. If this isn't the case, adjust the length of the rails and ledges as required.

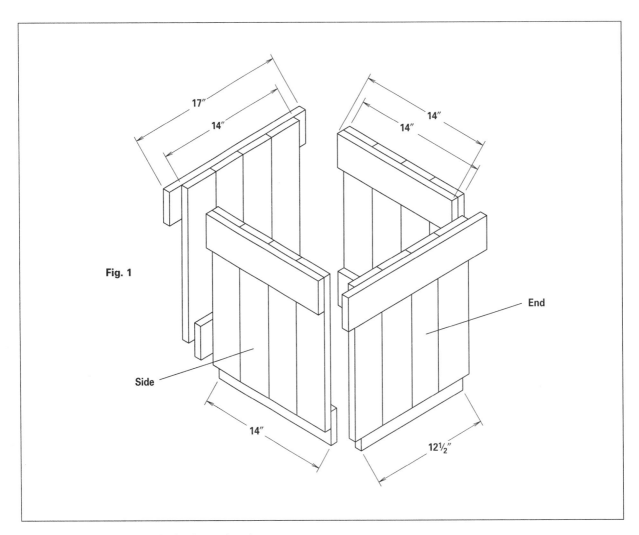

Illus. 6-58. Construction details for the garden planter.

SEESAW

Build this backyard toy (Illus. 6-59 and 6-60) for your children, and they are bound to get hours of fun out of it.

Tools and Materials Needed

- Handsaw
- Screwdriver
- Drill
- Jigsaw
- Threaded rod
- Washers
- Screws
- Captive nuts

Illus. 6-59. Seesaw.

Cutting List

Part	Qty.	Dimensions	Material
Main beam	1	$3\frac{1}{2}$ x $3\frac{1}{2}$ x 96 inches	Cedar
Leg	2	$3\frac{1}{2}$ x $3\frac{1}{2}$ x 36 inches	Cedar
Seat	2	$1\frac{1}{2}$ x $7\frac{1}{4}$ x 12 inches	Cedar
Handle	2	2-inch-diameter x 14 inches	Hardwood
Handle holder	2	$1\frac{1}{2}$ x $7\frac{1}{4}$ x 12 inches	Cedar
Handle base	2	$1\frac{1}{2}$ x $3\frac{1}{2}$ x $10\frac{3}{4}$ inches	Cedar
Stand	2	$1\frac{1}{2}$ x $7\frac{1}{4}$ x 18 inches	Cedar
Stand stretcher	2	$1\frac{1}{2}$ x $3\frac{1}{2}$ x 14 inches	Cedar

INSTRUCTIONS

1. Cut out the parts with a handsaw.

2. On two corners of each seat, measure in $1\frac{1}{2}$ inches along each edge and join the points with a line (Fig. 2 in Illus. 6-60). Use a handsaw to cut off the corner, keeping to the outside of the line.

3. Along both edges of each stand, measure up $15\frac{1}{8}$ inches from the bottom, mark a 45-degree angle from this point to the top of the stand, and cut the corner off with a handsaw (Fig. 3 in Illus. 6-60). Round the top of each stand with a sanding block or jigsaw.

4. Hold both stands together and drill a $\frac{1}{2}$-inch hole all the way through both of them. The hole should be centered from side to side and should be $1\frac{1}{2}$ inches from the top of the stands.

5. Cut the handle holders by first marking a 4-inch diameter on the top corner of the handle and

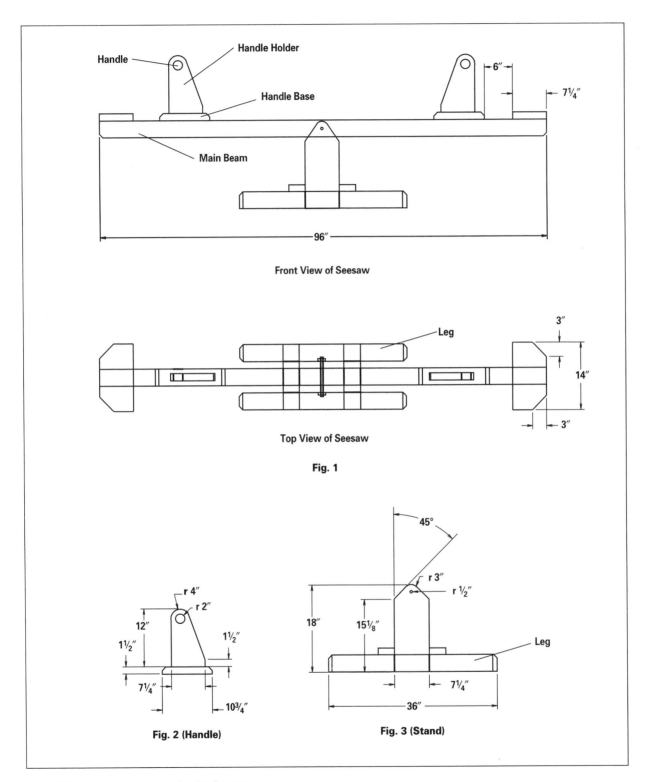

Front View of Seesaw

Top View of Seesaw

Fig. 1

Fig. 2 (Handle)

Fig. 3 (Stand)

Illus. 6-60. Construction details for the Seesaw.

drawing a line from the edge of this to within $1\frac{1}{2}$ inches of the bottom (Fig. 2 in Illus. 6-60). Cut along the straight line with a handsaw, and use a jigsaw to form the 4-inch-diameter radius.

6. Drill a 2-inch hole in the center of the 4-inch radius at the top of the handle holders to fit your 2-inch-diameter dowel. Position the dowel into the hole so that it is the same length on each side, and drill a countersunk pilot hole through the edge of the handle and into the dowel. Secure the dowel in place with a $1\frac{1}{2}$-inch-long screw.

7. Chamfer the top of the handle bases at each end with either a plane or handsaw.

8. Screw the base into the handle holder from underneath, using

Tip

• If you don't have a 2-inch drill bit to drill the hole for the handle, use the largest drill bit you have (it should be a minimum 1 inch) and buy a dowel to fit the hole. Remember that a hole saw won't allow you to drill all the way through the $1\frac{1}{2}$-inch-thick wood.

at least four 3-inch screws in countersunk pilot holes; make certain the handle is centered on the base.

9. Drill a $\frac{1}{2}$-inch hole through the main beam. The hole should be centered on the width and length of the beam.

10. Screw the seats and handle bases onto the main beam.

11. Chamfer the legs by cutting off their corners with a handsaw; then screw the stands to the legs so that the stands are centered and flush at the bottom (Fig. 3 in Illus. 6-60).

12. Screw the crosspieces onto the legs. Make sure the space between the stands is wide enough to accommodate the main beam.

13. Install the $\frac{1}{2}$-inch threaded rod through the $\frac{1}{2}$-inch hole in the stands and the main beam. Add a washer at each end and screw on captive nuts for safety.

References

• Pilot Holes in Chapter 2
• Using a Drill in Chapter 2
• Selecting Materials for Outdoor Projects in Chapter 4

COATRACK

Whether you use this coatrack (Illus. 6-61 and 6-62) for yourself or your children, it will keep things off the floor and within easy reach. For children, install it at their height so they can hang up their own coats.

Tools and Materials Needed

- Handsaw
- Drill
- Chamfering tool or sanding block
- Coat pegs

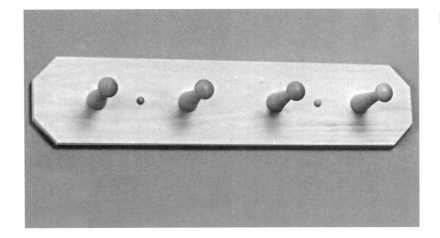

Illus. 6-61. Coatrack.

Cutting List

Part	Qty.	Dimensions	Material
Back	1	¾ x 5½ x 26 inches	Maple
Peg	4	4½ inches long	Hardwood

Tips

- You can make the coatrack as long or short as desired.
- Use a scroll saw to cut the backing board into a decorative shape.
- Instead of a chamfering tool or a sanding block, you can use a hand plane to make the chamfer.

INSTRUCTIONS

1. Cut the parts out with a handsaw.

2. Measure in 1 inch along the edge from each corner of the back piece and join the points. Cut off the corner with a handsaw, cutting to the outside of the line.

3. Chamfer all edges with a chamfering tool or a sanding block.

4. Using a ruler or tape measure, mark the center of the back piece at both ends, and then join the marks with a light line.

5. Measure 4, 7, and finally 10 inches in from each end and make a mark across the centerline to indicate the position for the holes.

6. Use a ¾-inch drill bit (or other size of drill bit to suit your pegs) to drill the peg holes all the way through at the 4- and 10-inch marks. Use a backing board to prevent splintering.

7. Drill the two counterbored pilot

holes at the 7-inch marks for mounting the coatrack.

8. Apply glue to the ends of the pegs and put them into the holes. Make sure the pegs are properly seated in the holes and are straight; then leave the assembly to dry.

References

- Using a Drill in Chapter 2
- Pilot Holes in Chapter 2
- Sanding and Finishing in Chapter 5

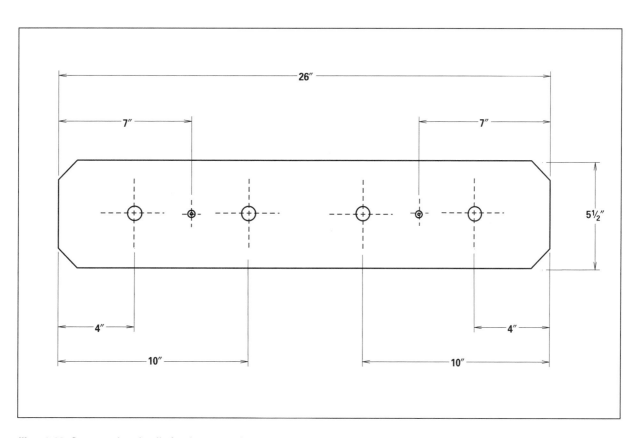

Illus. 6-62. Construction details for the coatrack.

RECIPE BOOK HOLDER

Use this recipe book holder (Illus. 6-63–6-65) to keep your favorite recipe book out of harm's way and at a better angle for reading while you create delicious meals in the kitchen.

Illus. 6-63. Recipe book holder.

Cutting List

Part	Qty.	Dimensions	Material
Back slat	2	$\frac{3}{4}$ x $1\frac{1}{2}$ x 16 inches	Pine
Back slat	1	$\frac{3}{4}$ x $5\frac{1}{2}$ x 16 inches	Pine
Ledge	1	$\frac{3}{4}$ x $1\frac{1}{2}$ x 16 inches	Pine
Leg	1	$\frac{3}{4}$ x $3\frac{1}{2}$ x 8 inches	Pine

Tools and Materials Needed

- Handsaw
- Screwdriver
- Hand plane or sanding block
- Hinges

INSTRUCTIONS

1. Cut the parts with a handsaw.

2. Take one of the $1\frac{1}{2}$-inch-wide back slats and measure $1\frac{1}{2}$ inches in from each end along one edge; make a mark at that point. Join this mark with the corner and cut off the waste.

3. Glue the three back slats together, making sure that the front and the edges of the recipe book holder are flush. Allow it to dry.

4. Chamfer one edge of the ledge with a hand plane or sanding block.

5. Glue the ledge to the back so that it is flush at the back edge and ends.

Illus. 6-64. The recipe book holder in use.

6. For the legs, measure 1 inch from each end of the board on opposite edges, and join those points. Cut along the center of the line with a handsaw.

7. Attach the legs to the back with hinges.

Tips
• You can make the holder longer or shorter, as desired.
• As a decorative feature and to make gluing up the back easier, chamfer the mating edges of the pieces before gluing them together.
• Use a miter box to cut the corner off the top back slat.
• Use a hand plane instead of a sanding block to chamfer the ledge.

References

• Gluing Up Boards in Chapter 3
• Miter Joints in Chapter 3
• Sanding and Finishing in Chapter 5

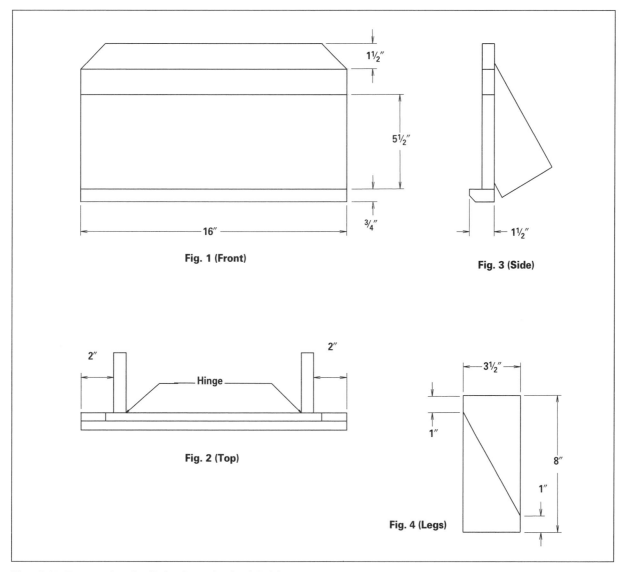

Fig. 1 (Front)

Fig. 3 (Side)

Fig. 2 (Top)

Fig. 4 (Legs)

Illus. 6-65. Construction details for the recipe book holder.

KITCHEN KEEPER

This project (Illus. 6-66–6-68) not only gives you a place to showcase some of your more attractive containers and kitchen accessories, it also helps end the clutter in your cupboards or drawers and keeps things within easy reach.

Tools and Materials Needed

- Handsaw
- Screwdriver
- Drill
- Screws
- Cup hooks

INSTRUCTIONS

1. Cut out the parts with a handsaw.

2. Measure 1 inch in from each end along one edge of the top and back pieces, connect the points, and cut the corner off at a 45-degree angle with a handsaw.

3. Drill three countersunk pilot holes in the back side of the back piece $1\frac{7}{8}$ inches from its top (Fig. 2 in Illus. 6-68).

4. For mounting the kitchen keeper, drill two counterbored pilot holes in the front of the back piece 3 inches in from the ends

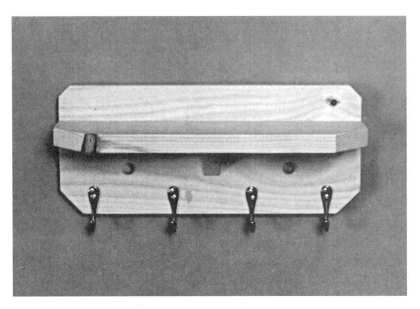

Illus. 6-66. Kitchen keeper.

Cutting List

Part	Qty.	Dimensions	Material
Top	1	$\frac{3}{4}$ x $3\frac{1}{2}$ x 13 inches	Pine
Back	1	$\frac{3}{4}$ x $5\frac{1}{2}$ x 13 inches	Pine
Brace	1	$\frac{3}{4}$ x $1\frac{1}{2}$ x $1\frac{1}{2}$ inches	Pine

Tip

- You can make the kitchen keeper longer, or even use wooden pegs instead of cup hooks.

Illus. 6-67. The kitchen keeper in use.

and 2½ inches up from the bottom.

5. Position the top piece against the back piece so its top surface is 1½ inches below the top of the back, and screw the pieces together.

6. Cut out the brace from a 1½-inch-wide board and glue it in place.

7. Screw four cup hooks to the kitchen keeper, evenly spaced 1½ inches up from the bottom.

References

- Pilot Holes in Chapter 2
- Miter Joints in Chapter 3
- Sanding and Finishing in Chapter 5

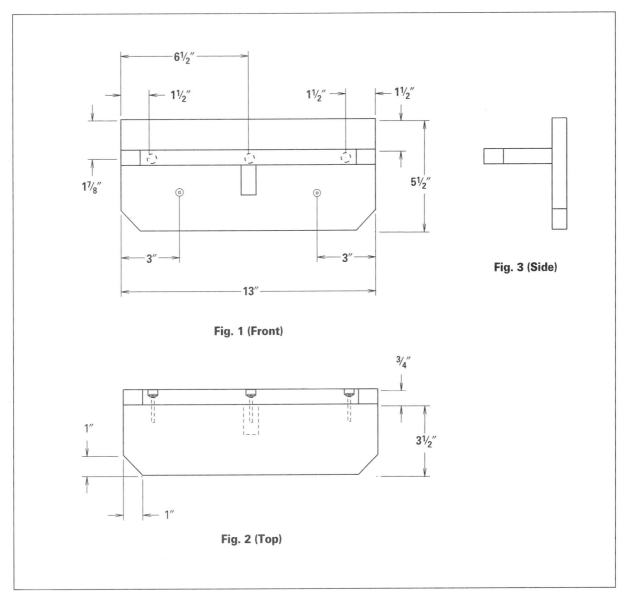

Fig. 1 (Front)

Fig. 2 (Top)

Fig. 3 (Side)

Illus. 6-68. Construction details for the kitchen keeper.

WORKBENCH

If you have room for a full-sized workbench, building your own will be more rewarding than buying one. This version (Illus. 6-69 and 6-70) is simple and inexpensive to build.

Illus. 6-69. Workbench.

Cutting List

Part	Qty.	Dimensions	Material
Stretcher	2	$1\frac{1}{2}$ x $3\frac{1}{2}$ x 40 inches	Pine
Leg	6	$1\frac{1}{2}$ x $3\frac{1}{2}$ x 33 inches	Pine
Back leg spacer (top)	2	$1\frac{1}{2}$ x $3\frac{1}{2}$ x 6 inches	Pine
Back leg spacer (middle)	2	$1\frac{1}{2}$ x $3\frac{1}{2}$ x 12 inches	Pine
Back leg spacer (bottom)	2	$1\frac{1}{2}$ x $3\frac{1}{2}$ x 8 inches	Pine
Base	2	$1\frac{1}{2}$ x $3\frac{1}{2}$ x 26 inches	Pine
Base center spacer	2	$1\frac{1}{2}$ x $3\frac{1}{2}$ x 13 inches	Pine
Base end cap	4	$1\frac{1}{2}$ x $3\frac{1}{2}$ x 3 inches	Pine
Top support	2	$1\frac{1}{2}$ x $1\frac{1}{2}$ x 20 inches	Pine
Top piece	2	$\frac{3}{4}$ x 24 x 48 inches	Plywood
Front/back skirt	2	$\frac{3}{4}$ x $1\frac{1}{2}$ x $53\frac{1}{2}$ inches	Maple
Side skirt	3	$\frac{3}{4}$ x $1\frac{1}{2}$ x 24 inches	Maple
Back panel	1	$\frac{1}{8}$ x 18 x 40 inches	Masonite
Tray bottom	1	$\frac{1}{8}$ x 6 x 27 inches	Masonite

Tools and Materials Needed

- Handsaw
- Hammer
- Screwdriver
- Drill
- Nails
- Washers and bolts

INSTRUCTIONS

1. Cut out the parts with a hand-saw.

2. To make the two front legs, glue up two leg pieces for each one, making sure they are flush on the ends and sides.

3. Make the back legs by gluing the leg spacers onto the leg piece (Fig. 1 in Illus. 6-70). The space between the spacers needs to accommodate the stretchers, so use a scrap piece in between the spacers when you glue them on. Start with the bottom 8-inch spacer, add a piece of scrap, and then add the 12-inch spacer. Add another scrap piece and, finally, the last 6-inch spacer. Trim the last spacer to size if necessary.

4. On each base end cap, cut the top edge off one end with a handsaw to make a large chamfer.

5. To make the base, first glue the end caps in place so they are flush at the ends of the base and on the side. To get the correct distance for the middle spacer, position the legs against the end

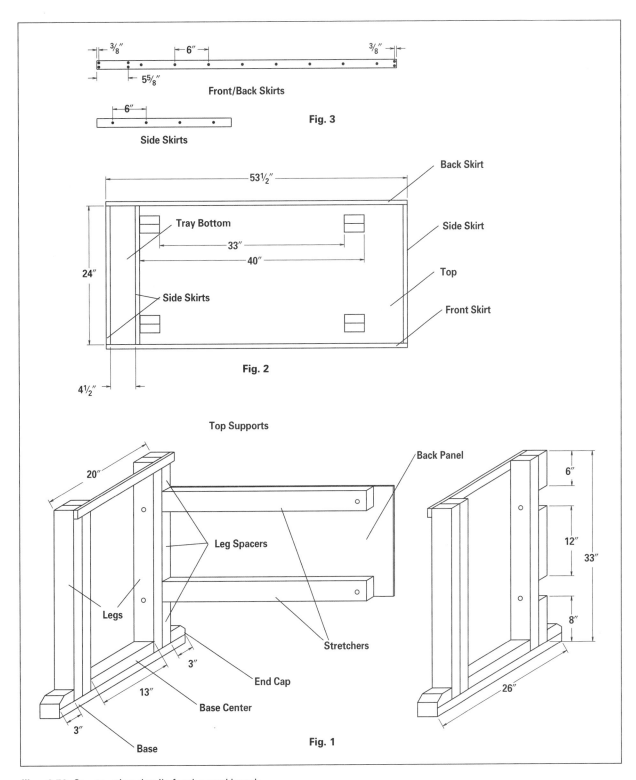

Illus. 6-70. Construction details for the workbench.

caps and measure between them. Cut out the middle spacer to fit, and glue it in position.

6. Attach the legs to the base by first gluing them in place, and then screwing them onto the base with 3-inch screws or lag bolts from underneath. Make sure that the spacers on the back legs are both facing the same way (Fig. 1 in Illus. 6-70).

7. Put the stretchers in place in the spaces on the back legs so that the legs are flush with the ends of the stretchers. Drill a $\frac{3}{4}$-inch hole $\frac{1}{2}$ inch into the back of the stretcher where the two pieces overlap; then drill a $\frac{3}{8}$-inch hole all the way through the stretchers and leg in the center of the $\frac{3}{4}$-inch hole. Put a $\frac{3}{8}$-inch washer in the $\frac{3}{4}$-inch hole, insert the bolt through the hole, add another washer with a nut on the other end, and tighten the bolt.

8. Screw the back panel in place over the stretchers and legs with $1\frac{1}{4}$-inch screws spaced about 3 inches apart and $1\frac{1}{2}$ inches in from the edge.

9. On one of the benchtop pieces, lay out a grid of 6-inch squares for the dog-holes. Flip it over and add the second benchtop piece so that their edges are flush. Screw the two together with $1\frac{1}{4}$-inch screws, making sure your screws are in the middle of each 6-inch square, not where the lines intersect.

10. Flip the benchtop over one more time and drill $\frac{3}{4}$-inch dog-holes at the intersection of each 6-inch square, making sure your hole is straight and at right angles to the benchtop. Use a backing board under each hole as you drill, to reduce splintering.

11. Drill the countersunk pilot holes in the front and back skirts and two end skirts. Drill matching pilot holes in the ends of the end skirts so that the screws won't split the wood then you assemble the skirts (Fig. 3 in Illus. 6-70).

12. Screw the three end skirts to the front skirt and place the benchtop inside the skirts with the top surface down. Screw the skirt to the edge of the benchtop through the pilot holes. Screw the back skirt to the end skirt and the edge of the benchtop.

13. Glue and nail the tray bottom to the underside of the tray with 1-inch nails.

14. Screw the two top supports to the legs. Then put the top in place and screw it on from underneath through the top supports.

> ***Tip***
>
> • You can make the legs from maple instead of pine.

References

- Pilot Holes in Chapter 2
- Using a Drill in Chapter 2
- Butt Joints in Chapter 3

ACTIVITY CENTER

Keep your child entertained with this activity center (Illus. 6-71 and 6-72). Tape paper to it, stock it with paint and crayons, and revel in your child's creativity.

Tools and Materials Needed

- Handsaw
- Screwdriver
- Drill
- Screws
- Nails
- Hinges
- Bolts

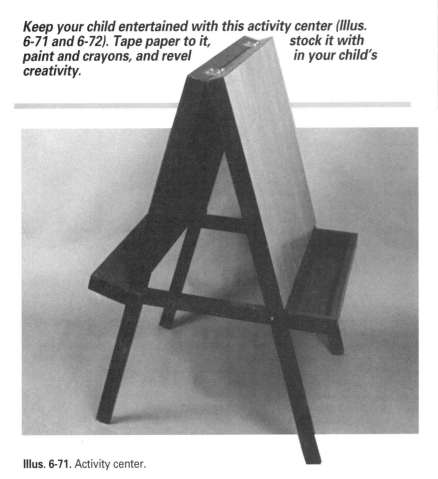

Illus. 6-71. Activity center.

Cutting List

Part	Qty.	Dimensions	Material
Leg	4	$3/4 \times 1\frac{1}{2} \times 42\frac{1}{4}$ inches	Pine
Crosspiece	4	$3/4 \times 1\frac{1}{2} \times 22\frac{1}{4}$ inches	Pine
Flat shelf crosspiece	2	$3/4 \times 1\frac{1}{2} \times 20\frac{7}{8}$ inches	Pine
Angled shelf crosspiece	2	$3/4 \times 1\frac{1}{2} \times 24$ inches	Pine
Angled shelf side	2	$3/4 \times 1\frac{1}{2} \times 6$ inches	Pine
Angled shelf top	1	$1/4 \times 4\frac{1}{2} \times 25\frac{1}{2}$ inches	Plywood
Flat shelf bottom	1	$1/4 \times 5\frac{1}{2} \times 22\frac{3}{8}$ inches	Plywood
Work surface	2	$1/4 \times 24 \times 23\frac{7}{8}$ inches	Plywood

INSTRUCTIONS

1. Cut out the parts with a handsaw.

2. Assemble the frames for each side of the activity center (Fig. 1 in Illus. 6-72) and drill two countersunk pilot holes through the legs and into each crosspiece. Apply glue to the mating surfaces and screw the pieces together.

3. Glue the work surfaces to the frames so that the top and both sides are flush. Trim the work surfaces with a sanding block or hand plane if necessary.

4. For the flat shelf (Fig. 4 in Illus. 6-72) and angled shelf, assemble the frames and drill two countersunk pilot holes through the sides and into each crosspiece. Apply glue to the mating surfaces and screw the pieces together.

5. Glue the angled shelf top to the angled shelf frame and the flat shelf bottom to the flat shelf frame, making sure they are flush with the frames. For extra strength, secure them with 1-inch nails.

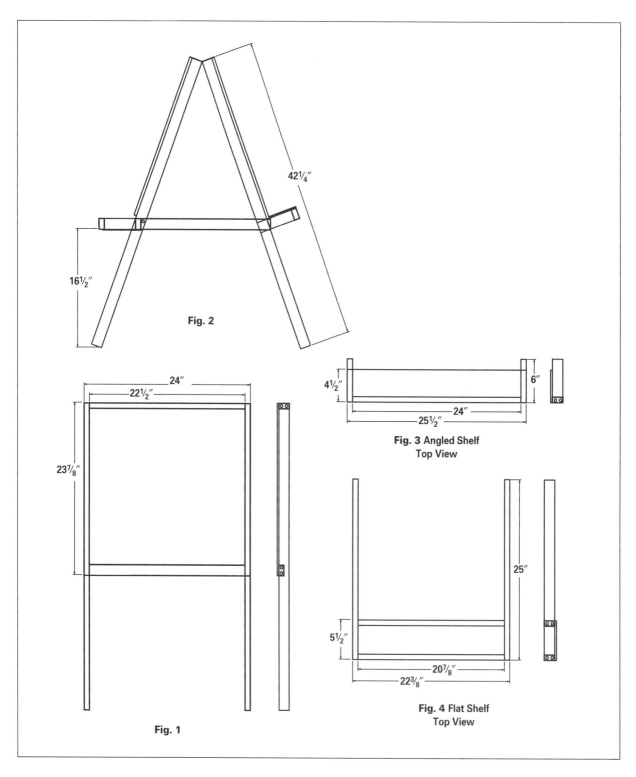

Fig. 2

42¼″

16½″

Fig. 1

24″

22½″

23⁷⁄₈″

4½″

25½″

24″

6″

**Fig. 3 Angled Shelf
Top View**

25″

5½″

20⁷⁄₈″

22³⁄₈″

**Fig. 4 Flat Shelf
Top View**

Illus. 6-72. Construction details for the activity center.

6. Position the flat shelf on one of the activity center frames so that the two work surfaces meet at a right angle; then drill two countersunk pilot holes in each side where the pieces overlap. Apply glue to the mating surfaces and screw the shelf in place.

7. Hold the two sides of the activity center together and screw on two hinges at the top.

8. Place the flat shelf in position (Fig. 2 in Illus. 6-72) with the activity center set up, and mark a line across the leg on each side, matching the top edge of the shelf frame. Measure down $3/8$ inch from this line and $3/8$ inch in from the inside edge of the leg. At this point, drill a $1/4$-inch hole through both the leg and shelf frame on both sides of the activity center. With a washer on each side, insert the $1/4$-inch bolt through the hole on each leg and secure the bolt with the nut. This will allow the ends of the shelf to swing up so the activity center can be folded flat.

Tips
• You can make the activity center wider, to accommodate more than one child per side.
• Use a miter box to cut the pieces square.

References

• Pilot Holes in Chapter 2
• Using a Drill in Chapter 2
• Sanding and Finishing in Chapter 5

SNACK TABLE

Whether you sit out on your porch or patio, you need something to rest your drink and snacks on. This attractive cedar table (Illus. 6-73 and 6-74) does the trick.

Tools and Materials Needed

- Handsaw
- Screwdriver
- Drill
- Jigsaw
- Screws

Illus. 6-73. Snack table.

Cutting List

Part	Qty.	Dimensions	Material
Top	3	$1\frac{1}{2}$ x $5\frac{1}{2}$ x $16\frac{1}{2}$ inches	Cedar
Feet	2	$1\frac{1}{2}$ x $5\frac{1}{2}$ x $13\frac{1}{4}$ inches	Cedar
Cross brace	2	$1\frac{1}{2}$ x $1\frac{1}{2}$ x 13 inches	Cedar
Leg	4	$1\frac{1}{2}$ x $1\frac{1}{2}$ x 20 inches	Cedar

INSTRUCTIONS

1. Cut out the parts with a handsaw.

2. Cut a 45-degree piece off both ends of two of the top pieces, starting $\frac{1}{2}$ inch from the edge so that you won't end up with a sharp corner (Fig. 2 in Illus. 6-74).

3. Cut a bevel on the ends of each cross brace with your handsaw (Fig. 1 in Illus. 6-74).

4. Place one cross brace on its side and position two legs on top of it so that their tops are flush with the top of the cross brace and their outside edges are $5\frac{1}{2}$ inches apart, centered on the cross brace. Drill two countersunk pilot holes where each piece overlaps, and screw the legs to the cross brace with two $2\frac{1}{2}$-inch screws. Repeat this with the other cross brace.

5. Lay out the tabletop pieces (Fig. 2 in Illus. 6-74) and position the cross braces, with the legs screwed to them, onto the tabletop. The cross braces should be $5\frac{1}{2}$ inches apart and centered on the tabletop. Where the cross brace overlaps each tabletop

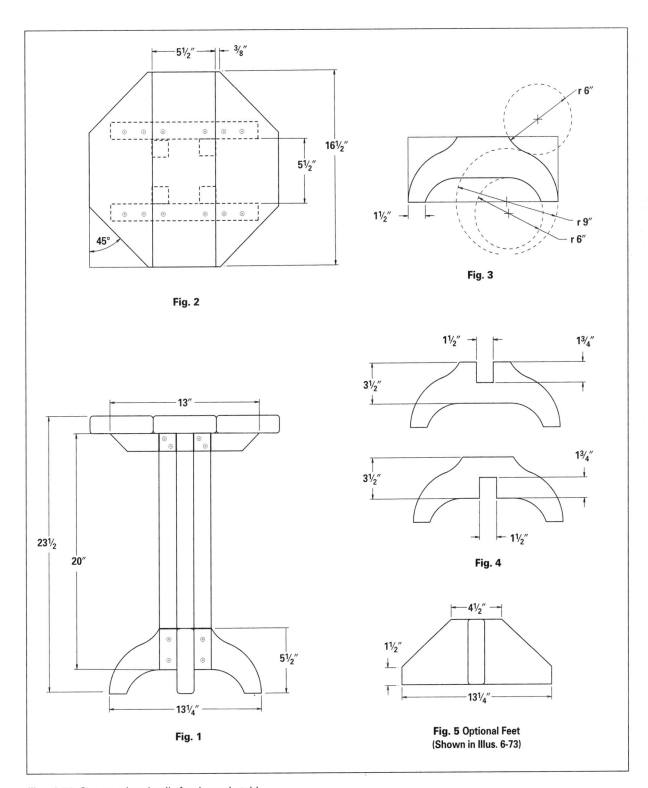

Illus. 6-74. Construction details for the patio table.

piece, drill two countersunk pilot holes in the cross brace and screw it to the tabletop.

6. Draw the curves on the feet (Fig. 3 in Illus. 6-74) and cut out the waste with a jigsaw.

7. On each foot, measure for the cross-lap joint and cut out the waste with a jigsaw. Test the fit of the foot and the leg and trim the openings as required with a handsaw or jigsaw.

8. Put the feet together and place them on the end of the legs. Drill countersunk pilot holes in the leg pieces and screw them onto the feet with 2½-inch screws.

References
- Pilot Holes in Chapter 2
- Lap Joints in Chapter 3
- Selecting Materials for Outdoor Projects in Chapter 4

Tip

- If you don't have a jigsaw or want a simpler foot, use the alternate foot shape shown in Fig. 5 of Illus. 6-74.

PATIO BENCH

This patio bench (Illus. 6-75 and 6-76) can be used on its own or with the snack table project. Build it to any length you want, either to suit a particular place on your patio or for the patio table itself.

Tools and Materials Needed

- Handsaw
- Drill
- Screws
- #100 sandpaper

Illus. 6-75. Patio bench.

Cutting List

Part	Qty.	Dimensions	Material
Seat slat	2	1½ x 5½ x 48 inches	Cedar
Seat end	2	1½ x 3½ x 11½ inches	Cedar
Leg	2	1½ x 5½ x 16½ inches	Cedar
Leg end	2	1½ x 3½ x 12 inches	Cedar
Leg-end cap	4	1½ x 3½ x 3¼ inches	Cedar
Crosspiece	1	1½ x 3½ x 14 inches	Cedar

INSTRUCTIONS

1. Cut the parts with a handsaw.

2. Place the seat pieces on the ground and space them ½ inch apart; then screw the seat ends in place with eight screws at each end, positioned so the screws won't be in the way when you cut the corner off.

3. Measure 1½ inches in from each corner and cut the corner piece off at a 45-degree angle with a handsaw (Fig. 1 in Illus. 6-76).

4. Place the leg ends on the ground and position the legs on top of them so that they are flush on the bottom and centered from side to side. Put the leg-end caps in place on each end and screw them on with three screws positioned so they won't be in the way when you cut the corner off. Trim the end caps to length if required.

5. Remove the legs and cut the corners off the leg ends at a 45-degree angle at each end with a handsaw.

6. Put the legs back in place on the leg ends, screwing them on and using four screws for each leg.

147

7. Screw the legs onto the seat ends.

8. Measure and cut the crosspiece to length, position it halfway up the legs, and screw it in place through the legs with two screws at each end.

9. Sand all the edges of the boards smooth with #100 sandpaper.

Reference

• Selecting Materials for Outdoor Projects in Chapter 4

Tips

• You can make the bench longer or shorter, as desired.
• For this project, you will want to use your drill and power-driver bits to drive the screws.
• Drill countersunk pilot holes, to ensure easy assembly and to reduce splintering.

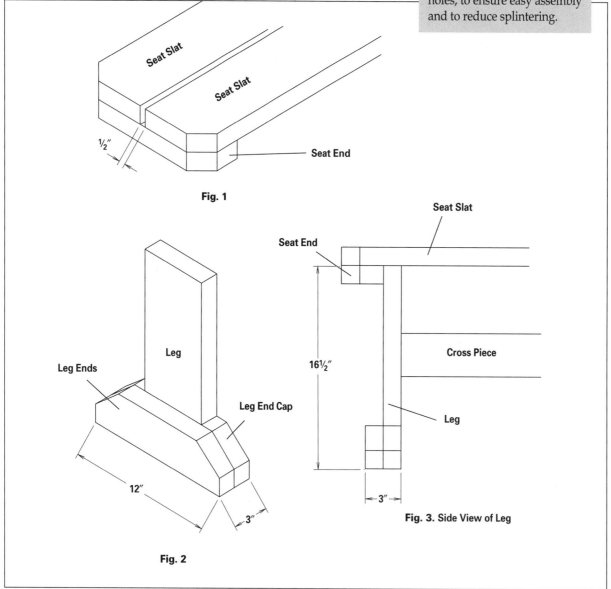

Illus. 6-76. Construction details for the patio bench.

PATIO TABLE

This table (Illus. 6-77–6-79) makes an attractive alternative to a picnic table or store-bought patio tables. Build the patio bench (pages 147 and 148) to accompany this project.

Tools and Materials Needed

• Handsaw
• Drill
• Screws
• #100 sandpaper

Illus. 6-77. Patio table.

Cutting List

Part	Qty.	Dimensions	Material
Top	5	1½ x 5½ x 60 inches	Cedar
Long support	4	1½ x 3½ x 40 inches	Cedar
Cross support	5	1½ x 3½ x 30 inches	Cedar
Foot pad	4	1½ x 3½ x 3½ inches	Cedar
Center post (A)	2	1½ x 7¼ x 16 inches	Cedar
Center post (B)	2	1½ x 3½ x 23½ inches	Cedar
Stabilizer	4	1½ x 3½ x 5 inches	Cedar

INSTRUCTIONS

1. Cut the parts with a handsaw.

2. Cut a 45-degree piece off both ends of the two tabletop pieces, starting ½ inch from the edge so that you won't end up with a sharp corner (Illus. 6-78).

3. On the ends of each long support and on two cross supports, measure 2 inches from an edge along one end and mark a 45-degree line from this point. Cut off the corner by sawing to the outside of this line.

4. Screw the foot pads to the ends of two cross supports and cut a bevel on both ends of each one. Make sure your screws won't be in the way of the cut. (Illus. 6-79).

5. Assemble the center post by screwing the two 2 x 4s onto one 2 x 8 so that the 2 x 4s extend exactly 3½ inches beyond the 2 x 8 at both ends. Screw on the remaining 2 x 8 so that it is flush with the first 2 x 8.

6. Screw two long supports onto the 2 x 4 pieces extending from each end of the center post so that the long supports are centered end to end.

7. Screw three cross supports centered on top of one set of long supports so that those supports with beveled ends are at each end and a plain cross support is in the middle (Illus. 6-79).

8. Screw the two cross supports with the foot pads to the other set of long supports, one at each end, so they are centered.

9. Place the 5-inch-long stabilizers between the long supports against the cross supports at the top and bottom and screw them to the cross supports so they are flush with the top of the long supports. Drive two screws through the long supports into the 5-inch pieces from each side.

10. Lay out the tabletop pieces on the ground so that the best side of each board is facing down. Position the pieces with the 45-degree cuts on each side (Illus. 6-78).

11. Place the table leg assembly on top of the tabletop pieces so the three cross supports are centered on the boards. Screw the

cross supports into each board. Use at least two screws where each cross support overlaps a tabletop piece.

12. Sand all the edges of the boards smooth with #100 sandpaper.

Tips

• You can leave the tabletop square, if desired.
• For this project, you will want to use your drill and power-driver bits to drive the screws.
• Drill countersunk pilot holes for easy assembly and to reduce splintering.

Reference

• Selecting Materials for Outdoor Construction in Chapter 4

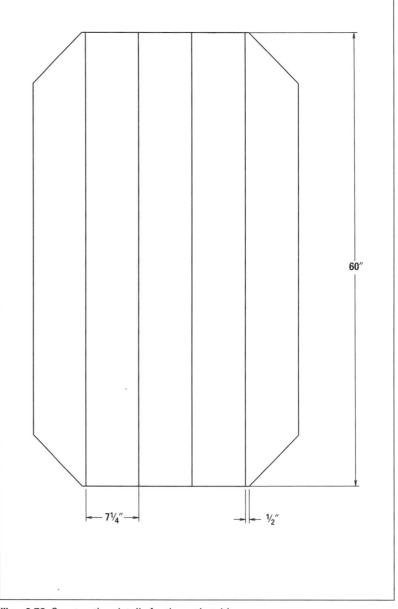

Illus. 6-78. Construction details for the patio table.

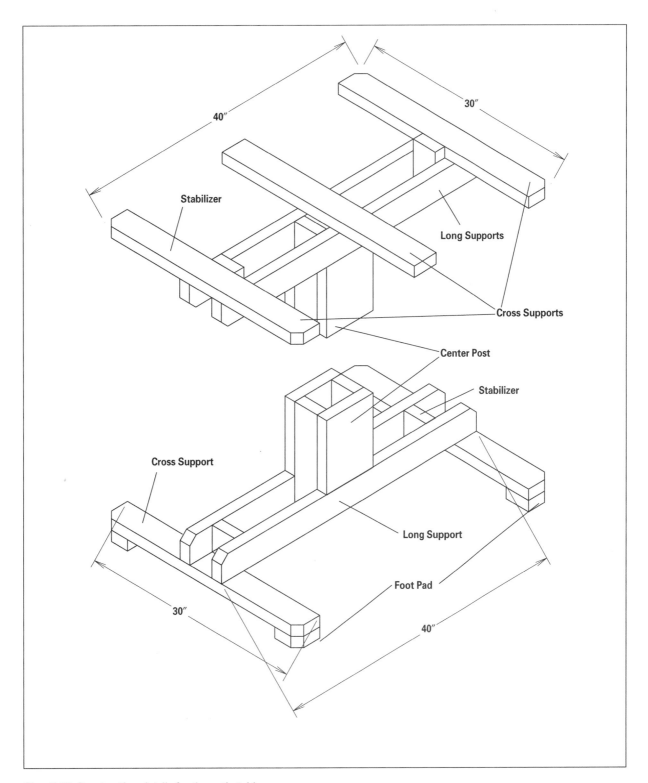

Illus. 6-79. Construction details for the patio table.

STEP STOOL

For young children, this step stool (Illus. 6-80 and 6-81) is ideal for the washroom so they can reach the sink. For adults, it can give that extra lift necessary for the top shelf of a bookshelf, pantry, or the kitchen cupboards.

Tools and Materials Needed

Handsaw
Screwdriver
Drill
Screws
Glue

Illus. 6-80. Step stool.

Cutting List

Part	Qty.	Dimensions	Material
Tall side	4	$3/4$ x $3\frac{1}{2}$ x 11 inches	Pine
Short side	2	$3/4$ x $5\frac{1}{2}$ x $5\frac{1}{2}$ inches	Pine
High top	2	$3/4$ x $3\frac{1}{2}$ x 12 inches	Pine
Low top	1	$3/4$ x $5\frac{1}{2}$ x 12 inches	Pine
Low support	4	$3/4$ x $1\frac{1}{2}$ x 11 inches	Pine
Short support	2	$3/4$ x $1\frac{1}{2}$ x $5\frac{1}{2}$ inches	Pine
Lower front	1	$3/4$ x $5\frac{1}{2}$ x $10\frac{1}{2}$ inches	Pine
Upper front	1	$3/4$ x $5\frac{1}{2}$ x $10\frac{1}{2}$ inches	Pine

INSTRUCTIONS

1. Cut out the parts with a handsaw.

2. Position the three pieces for each side of the step stool face-down on the workbench and lay the three crosspieces in place. Make sure that you have a matched set, and that the best faces of your boards are facing down. Drill countersunk pilot holes through the crosspieces and then screw them in place.

3. Turn the side pieces over and mark the centers for the two holes. Drill the holes out using a hole saw in your drill. Place a scrap backing piece underneath, to prevent splintering.

4. Drill counterbored pilot holes into the front edges of the side pieces $3/8$ inch from the edge. Do the same thing for the three step pieces.

5. Apply glue to the mating surfaces and screw the side pieces to the upper and lower front pieces, making sure they are flush at the top and the front.

6. Do the same for the step pieces.

7. Glue flat screw-hole plugs into the screw holes and sand them flush.

References

- Pilot Holes in Chapter 2
- Screw-Hole Plugs in Chapter 2
- Sanding and Finishing in Chapter 5

Tips

- You can use dowels instead of screws.
- You can cut out a decorative shape with your jigsaw instead of drilling the large holes in the sides.
- Use the edge of a front piece as a spacer while screwing the crosspieces to the sides, to make sure you leave enough room.

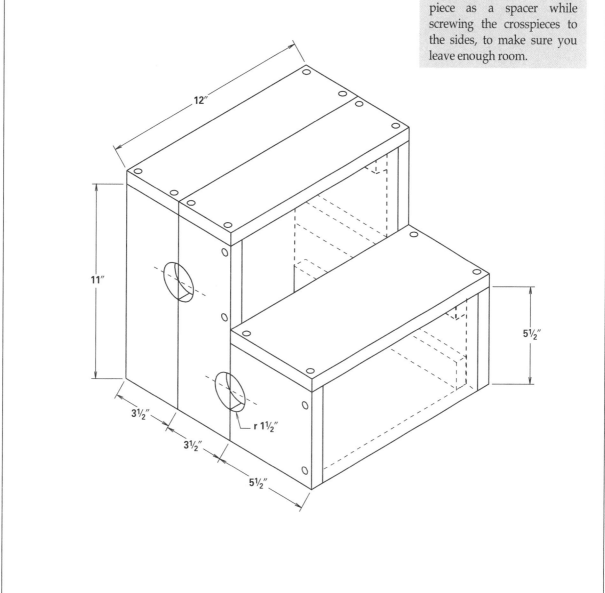

Illus. 6-81. Construction details for the step stool.

SPOON RACK

If you collect spoons or know someone who does, then this project (Illus. 6-82 and 6-83) will provide an easy-to-make solution for displaying them. Whether it holds your entire collection or a select group of them, it will look great on your wall.

Tools and Materials Needed

- Handsaw
- Hammer
- Drill
- Miter box
- Finishing nails
- Glue

Illus. 6-82. Spoon rack.

Cutting List

Part	Qty.	Dimensions	Material
Side	2	³⁄₄ x 1¹⁄₂ x 20 inches	Pine
Top/bottom	2	³⁄₄ x 1¹⁄₂ x 12 inches	Pine
Spoon holder	4	³⁄₄ x 1¹⁄₂ x 12 inches	Pine
Face frame top/bottom	2	³⁄₄ x 1¹⁄₂ x 13¹⁄₂ inches	Pine
Face frame side	2	³⁄₄ x 1¹⁄₂ x 20 inches	Pine

INSTRUCTIONS

1. Cut out the parts with a handsaw.

2. Take the four 12-inch-long spoon holder pieces and draw a line ¹⁄₂ inch from one edge on their top faces.

3. Mark this line 1¹⁄₂ inches in from each side. Then mark 1¹³⁄₁₆ inches in from this line, repeating twice for each side to get six evenly spaced marks.

4. Drill a ³⁄₈-inch hole all the way through at each mark, using a backing board underneath the piece to prevent splintering.

5. Make two perpendicular lines on the top of the pieces at each hole ¹⁄₄ inch apart from each other and centered on each hole.

6. Cut to the inside of these lines with a handsaw. (See Tips.)

7. Nail the top and bottom and four spoon shelves to the side pieces.

8. Cut the miters on the face-frame pieces.

9. Glue the face-frame pieces onto the box and tack in place with finishing nails.

References
• Using a Drill in Chapter 2
• Miter Joints in Chapter 3
• Sanding and Finishing in Chapter 5

Tips
• Use a jigsaw instead of a hand-saw to cut the openings for the spoons.
• When cutting the molding to frame the spoon rack, cut one side, lay it on the project, and measure exactly for the miter cut on the other end.
• Drill pilot holes for the nails, to reduce the possibility of splitting.

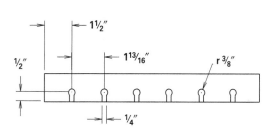

Fig. 1

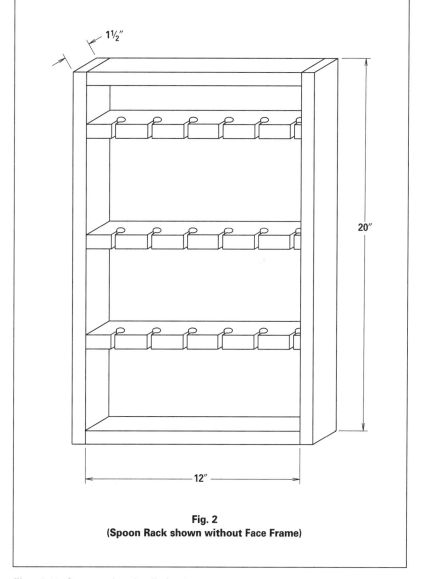

Fig. 2
(Spoon Rack shown without Face Frame)

Illus. 6-83. Construction details for the spoon rack.

UNDER-THE-BED DRAWER

Make use of the space under your bed with this stand-alone drawer (Illus. 6-84 and 6-85). It rolls under your bed on its own wheels, eliminating the need for drawer guides or a frame.

Illus. 6-84. Under-the-bed drawer.

Cutting List

Part	Qty.	Dimensions	Material
Drawer back	1	$3/4$ x $5\frac{1}{2}$ x $23\frac{3}{4}$ inches	Pine
Sides	2	$3/4$ x $5\frac{1}{2}$ x $23\frac{3}{4}$ inches	Pine
Drawer front	1	$3/4$ x $5\frac{1}{2}$ x $19\frac{1}{4}$ inches	Pine
Wheel support	2	$1\frac{1}{2}$ x $1\frac{1}{2}$ x $23\frac{3}{4}$ inches	Pine
Drawer support	4	$3/4$ x $3/4$ x 19 inches	Pine
Drawer bottom	1	$1/2$ x $19\frac{1}{4}$ x $23\frac{3}{4}$ inches	Plywood
Drawer face	1	$3/4$ x $5\frac{1}{2}$ x $23\frac{3}{4}$ inches	Pine
Wheel	4	$1\frac{1}{4}$-inch-diameter with mounting plate	

Tools and Materials Needed

- Handsaw
- Screwdriver
- Drill
- Drawer pull
- Wheels
- Screws
- Glue

INSTRUCTIONS

1. Cut out the parts with a handsaw.

2. Drill countersunk pilot holes in the center and in each end of the drawer supports. Screw the supports to the front, back, and side drawer pieces so they are centered side to side and flush at the bottom, as shown in Fig. 1 in Illus. 6-85.

3. Drill two countersunk pilot holes $3/8$ inch in from one end of the side pieces and $3/4$ inch from the top and bottom edges. Then apply glue to the mating surfaces and screw the side pieces to the front piece.

4. Lay out this assembly with the back piece in place so that it overhangs $1\frac{1}{2}$ inches on each side. Make sure the side pieces are square to the front, and mark the location of the countersunk holes in the back piece. Drill the countersunk pilot holes, apply glue, and screw the back to the sides.

5. Attach the drawer pull to the drawer face using the instructions included with the drawer pull. Then attach the drawer face

to the drawer front from the inside by drilling four counter-sunk pilot holes on the inside of the drawer and screwing the drawer front in place.

6. Screw the 1½ x 1½-inch side rails to the side from the inside through countersunk pilot holes (Fig. 2 in Illus. 6-85).

7. Screw the wheels in place on the side rail (Fig. 3 in Illus. 6-85).

8. Insert the bottom into the drawer.

References

• Pilot Holes in Chapter 2

Tips

• Make the drawer wider, nar-rower, or longer, depending on your needs.
• The height of the side rails will depend on the wheels you buy. Be sure to allow ½ inch of clear-ance under the drawer.

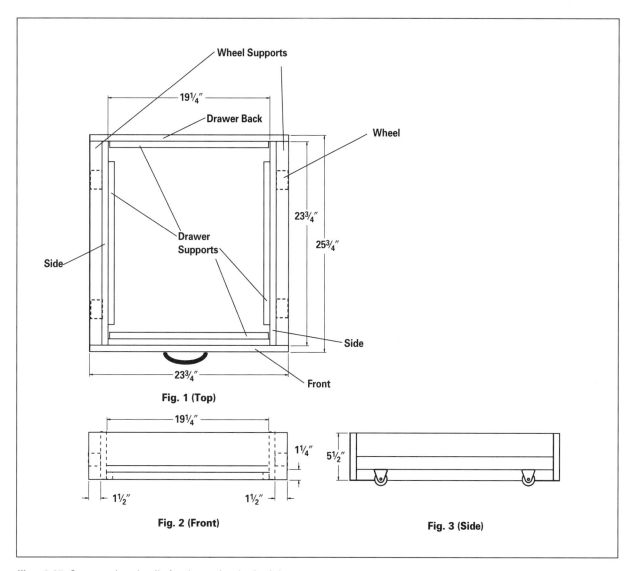

Fig. 1 (Top)

Fig. 2 (Front)

Fig. 3 (Side)

Illus. 6-85. Construction details for the under-the-bed drawer.

Metric Conversion Table
INCHES TO MILLIMETERS AND CENTIMETERS
MM—millimeters   *CM—centimeters*

Inches	MM	CM	Inches	CM	Inches	CM
⅛	3	0.3	9	22.9	30	76.2
¼	6	0.6	10	25.4	31	78.7
⅜	10	1.0	11	27.9	32	81.3
½	13	1.3	12	30.5	33	83.8
⅝	16	1.6	13	33.0	34	86.4
¾	19	1.9	14	35.6	35	88.9
⅞	22	2.2	15	38.1	36	91.4
1	25	2.5	16	40.6	37	94.0
1¼	32	3.2	17	43.2	38	96.5
1½	38	3.8	18	45.7	39	99.1
1¾	44	4.4	19	48.3	40	101.6
2	51	5.1	20	50.8	41	104.1
2½	64	6.4	21	53.3	42	106.7
3	76	7.6	22	55.9	43	109.2
3½	89	8.9	23	58.4	44	111.8
4	102	10.2	24	61.0	45	114.3
4½	114	11.4	25	63.5	46	116.8
5	127	12.7	26	66.0	47	119.4

INDEX